PRAIS
CRY THE WO

The conversations with God in *Cry the Wounded Land* are precious and important insights into his heart; for us as individuals, for our families, for our nation; for all nations! And woven throughout is the heart of God for the restoration of a conversational relationship with us. A conversation that has the ability to heal, mould and change us.

Libby Huirua. Author. Songwriter. Teacher.

Mark's unique talks with God in *The Freedom Diaries*, became a series of conversational exchanges well worth listening to. *Cry the Wounded Land* is an even more searching talk at an even more significant time.

Winkie Pratney. Author, International Bible Teacher.

Mark's writings come to him as direct revelations. That's what makes *Cry the Wounded Land* so intriguing - he knows very little of our Māori history and doesn't pretend to have all the answers. Yet he's a genuine bloke, and a mate, and now he's using his gift to bring understanding. It may help to reveal to our beautiful Pākehā Whānau, the perspective that some of us Māori have, of the predominantly Pākehā style of Church in Aotearoa, New Zealand today.

Norm McLeod. Māori. Founding pastor, House of Breakthrough.

I am excited about the pages of this book being read throughout our beautiful little nation. I believe it will stir an awareness, and value, for the song the land is singing. May we all discover the joy of falling in love with each other and with the very land we walk on. As it reads in the pages of this book, the very land is alive, and we have an opportunity which will change the course of history for generations to come!

Josh Klinkenberg. Christian Recording Artist. Author.

There is a huge gulf between religious performance, and the face to face intimacy of the kind Mark enjoys in *Cry the Wounded Land*. Like any relationship there is passion, fire, raw emotion and sometimes tears. And just as most of the wounds discussed in these pages have come through relationship, so too will their healing. I commend Mark for his courage in sharing such intimate communication and invite you to join him in the wild adventure of conversation with God.

Daniel Walker. Author – God in a Brothel.

Our only hope to heal the wounds in our nations, our lands and our hearts, is to hear God's voice. Mark is listening. I encourage you to read his conversations about Māori and Pākehā with an open mind and then, most importantly, go have a conversation with God yourself. We need supernatural insight on the explosive subject of race relations and it is essential that we hear God's heart. We must have Heaven's perspective, and that is exactly what Mark offers in this book.

Dr. Charity Virkler Kayembe. Author – Hearing God Through Your Dreams.

I so identify with Mark in this book. He questions, doubts and drags his heels, while God gently but repeatedly encourages him to see and understand the reasons He brought both of us, Māori and Pākehā, to New Zealand. This book touches my spirit. It is a conversation [with God] of poetic power and insight. It traces the potential of two peoples who can become a united warrior force that overturns darkness, and demonstrates the wisdom of God to the nations.

Graham Braddock. Renown New Zealand artist and Church Elder.

I agree one thousand percent with the following comment God makes in *Cry the Wounded Land* – "No more grovelling, now it's time for action. We have business to do, Māori, Pākehā and God working together. We need to get on with it. Each of you need to acknowledge the horror you have inflicted on others in this land – and then help each other to fix the mess."

Rangitikehu Paul. Kaumatua. Te Teko

I highly recommend these pages for weeping prophets, apostles of hope, tender teachers, edifying evangelists and passionate pastors. I have walked for 20 years with the custodians of a dream for the First Nations and Migrant Peoples of Australia. Mark's chapter, 'Back to the Beaches' shows us too, a place where we can step into the future. This book will have a thousand applications for First Nations, and dominant migration cultures in every country.

Tom Hallas. YWAM Field Director Asia and Pacific. YWAM Founders Circle.

Wow, what a powerful book! I read it on a flight to Europe and it got me crying at 10km up! This is brilliant, people need to read it. This conversation lies at the heart of our nation and the healing of our soul. The time is now! Let's truly listen...

Gideon Hoekendijk. Senior Pastor. Harmony Church.

The korero (conversation) with God in this book is both pono (true) and tika (correct). It is not just the land [Aotearoa] that got wounded, so did people. Many carry those wounds today. Some of those wounded hearts will be captured by this korero. And so the healing will begin. We must learn to walk, not just gently on the land, but also wisely because time is short. God has me doing something similar in Tuhoe, taking the word to the Marae, praying over the land and especially the Urupa, because of all the lost souls and children who were hurt by my own people with abuse. Congratulations, Mark, on a conversation with God that gives a lot of insight to man, no matter what colour, race or creed.

Te Tokaia Nohotima. Kaumatua. Te Kakano O Te Aroha Marae. Petone.

This book will either make or break you. Hopefully, when you read it, you will see we cannot remain the same. In our own spiritual journey over 30 years, we have noticed a paradigm shift, a unifying desire to grow in understanding God, the world, and each other. Two mighty nations, Māori and Pākehā, drawn by God's spirit, to this land of Aotearoa New Zealand (Acts 17:26-27). He wants us to partner with each other, not be divided. In these pages, Mark lays it out openly and tells it like it is, by having back and forward conversations with the mighty creator of the universe – in such a simple provoking way that cuts to the core of the heart.

Whare and Virginia Heta. Kaumātua. Nga Hau E Wha Marae.

Genuine, raw and humbling korero between Mark and God, shaping the future of Aotearoa... a must-read.

Matt and Rachel Renata. National Leadership. Baptist Māori Ministries.

I'm so grateful for the healing that comes from the things spoken of between Mark and our Lord. I cried over my own wounds of the past and present as I read *Cry the Wounded Land.* Only to have my tears wiped away by the journey of reconciliation that is flowing to unite Māori and Pākehā to make us One. Because the Lord, and the redeemed of the Lord say so!

Angel Taylor. Prophet and Teacher. Tangata Whenua Aotearoa.

Mark has had a big impact on me, and all of us at YWAM Oxford. The ability to hear God in a real conversation was something we were certain could happen, but through his and Miriam's story, we have experienced it. *Cry the Wounded Land* is God's conversation with Mark about the wound of Pākehā and Māori. If we have the courage to take over and keep this conversation going with God ourselves, what healing and unity might take place! Thanks for stepping out in front, Mark.

James Smith. YWAM Base Leader.

Cry the Wounded Land is a timely book for the message of unity and the blessing of God that can come from people being together. Reading these pages will remind people that God is interested in all areas of our lives, and that He is always willing to discuss the 'big issues' with us. I felt so encouraged reading this book and know you will too. So helpful and life-giving.

Taka Kauri. Youth Pastor, Hope Centre.

Cry the Wounded Land is heartfelt conversation, natural and raw, with God himself. It's a wake-up call. Hearing God is the most productive and important thing we can do! It confirms who we are, not what we think we are, or what we are told by others. It's the same for people groups, not just individuals! We all have a destiny which is unique and amazing, but can only be unlocked by listening to God. This book will give you the ability to confidently approach conversations with God, with expectations of solutions.

Nathan Buxton. Real Estate Agent.

Thought provoking and confronting! Mark's God conversations will make you question everything you thought you knew about the relationship between Māori and Pākehā, and subsequently God's purpose for our two diverse yet interconnected peoples.

HineKoia Tomlinson. Program Director. Excel School of Performing Arts.

There really should be something equivalent to a Government Health Warning to anyone picking up and reading this book! It will change how you exchange with others, should you take the challenge! The North and South Islands are different, so I sense our medicine [for these ills] will be differently applied and taken ...

Rev Dr Bryden Black. Theologian. Owner Mendip Hills Sheep Station.

"The way we see the problem is the problem", that's exactly what these conversations dive into head first. They bring fresh perspective to a complex issue. You're left with the unmistakable impression you've been conversing with God. If we're honest, Mark's questions to God are our own questions on these matters. These conversations are a breath of fresh air and a source of hope for our two great races.

Wayne Todd. Director. The Hub.

Mark's first book, *The Freedom Diaries,* literally changed my life, it opened a conversion with my greatest friend...God. Now this new book, *Cry the Wounded Land*, will change many more lives, should there be men and women brave enough to listen. It takes courage beyond imagination to bring a message from God as controversial as this book.

Gary Vaughan. Civil Machinery Operator.

Since reading *The Freedom Diaries*, God has taught me so much about relationship. In my conversations with God, I've listened to how he relates with me, and applied it to my relationship with my wife. It's changed our marriage! So now, as I read *Cry the Wounded Land*, I am ecstatic that God is pursuing this 'Māori, Pākehā and the Land' agenda. I love that he is not just talking kiss-and-make-up, but addressing what we really think and feel. I'm excited to see what happens when humans seek relationship across cultures, not just our own agenda. It's not OK to live fragmented! God wants to restore, are we listening?

Jeremy Stephenson. African People Photographer.

"In order to go forwards, sometimes you have to go backwards - back to the beginning - where our two cultures first met." Through conversing with God, Mark challenges our thinking and our responsibility for two cultures to become one, melded together, a mighty force. "One can put a thousand to flight, but two can put ten thousand to flight...." Deut 32:30

Pam Highsted. Christian Event Coordinator.

When I read these beautifully raw and transparent conversations between God and Mark, I felt included. The irony is that I was, I am, and so are you. *Cry the Wounded Land* is a must-read if you are passionate, or pondering about our Heavenly Father's thoughts. Especially His thoughts and desires about us, his children, and about connecting cultures in Aotearoa, New Zealand. Let's all hear God speak clearly on this topic, and lets all pursue unity and whakawhanaungatanga (relationship, relating well to each other).

Laraine Obrien, Te Anau.

Cry the Wounded Land is a challenging title. I try and look at New Zealanders as a mono-society - this is not a general concept, but I believe it needs to be. There have been let downs in our society. We are wounded. We need to talk to God and ask him the best way to bless and fix these let downs and wounds, whichever side we are on! To God we are one people and he loves us all deeply. God wants healing and love for our whole people. Mark, thank you for your special book. Thank you for challenging and uplifting our people.

Bob Wickham. Retired Farmer. Property Developer.

Cry the Wounded Land is a genuine transcript of Mark's ongoing conversations with "Papa". It is both exciting and challenging to think that "Papa" may be wanting the two peoples of Aotearoa to heal relationally, and become a beacon for the other nations.

Rob Hawley. Physics, Science and Technology Teacher.

Cry the Wounded Land is a call for Māori and Pākehā to work together in a way that God had always intended. Two peoples called to use each other's strengths, and create something in New Zealand that would be an example to the rest of the world. Here at Excel School of Performing Arts, God is bringing young Māori, Pākehā and Pacific artists together in a truly unique way. We have been exploring how our cultures can combine to produce songs, dance, drama – a unique expression of what God has always intended for this nation. The conversations in this book capture the heart of that...we're just outworking it in the performing arts. These are exciting times.

John Knight. Principal. Excel School of Performing Arts.

If you care about Aotearoa, then *Cry the Wounded Land* is a worthwhile investment. But be warned, it has the potential to strip you down, challenge you and make you look very deep into yourself and what you believe, about yourself and our nation. I invite you on this journey because we are in a time to bring about the healing that God always intended for us, as brothers, Māori and Pākehā, to walk together into the destiny God planned for us.

Jon McKenzie. Police Detective and Church Elder.

Main book starts page 43

Cry the Wounded Land

Conversations with God about Māori, Pākehā and the Land

MARK HOLLOWAY

Main book starts page 43

Cry the Wounded Land

Conversations with God about Māori, Pākehā and the Land.

Published by The Freedom Assignment Limited
First Printing September 2017

Editing Advisor: Dr Rossi Holloway

Cover: Blake Weston

ISBN: 978-0-473-39815-6

The Freedom Assignment Limited
www.thefreedomassignment.com
info@thefreedomdiaries.co.nz

Dedication

To my Māori brothers and sisters. Thank you.

For listening. For reading these pages.
Even though my colour says theft to you,
hate to you, a deaf ear to you.
Thank you for reading all the same.

I am not like you, and you are not like me.
I am so glad of that. Your colour inspires me, moves me when you shout, stomp and thunder. Thrills me when I read of your exploits.
Oh, that my colour might one day do the same for you.
Difference is what makes us strong.

When we do our difference together, we are indomitable and feared - on the sports field, in war, in music, marriage, entertainment, in business, finance, the arts and literature.

To my Pākehā blood brothers, and sisters. Thank you for reading too.
These pages may not be easy for you.

Some of you know these things already, the reading will touch spots already raw. Some of you don't know this yet, for you the reading may seem wrong, unfair.

It seemed that way to me too. At first anyway. Wrong. Unfair. Biased.
After all I'm like you. Pākehā.

But they're not, they're Māori. Yet God made us both, to be together.

And to the rest of you, every colour and religion.
You got here after us, and we after them.
Thank you for putting up with the two of us,
as we have warred and hated.
We are your two dysfunctional older brothers.
Please stick with us a little longer.
We will work this out. Somehow we will. We promise.

Mark.

PS: And thanks to you too, the Land, Aotearoa, New Zealand.
I can feel you ache and groan, longing for us to get our mess sorted.
Neither of us innocent, both to blame. Please wait a little longer.

Conversations

Foreword (Brad Haami. Māori) 15

Foreword (David Garratt. Pākehā) 19

Why this book? 23

Important insights from respected others 27

Conversations with God about Māori, Pākehā and the Land

1. Cry the Wounded Land 43
2. When you destroy their culture, you also destroy your own .. 53
3. A wild and fierce band of brothers! 57
4. A story of two people with blood on their hands. 63
5. 'In the bonds of love we meet.' Oh really? 71
6. Māori and Pākehā: Neither is complete without the other 79
7. Māori and Pākehā alive right now have an opportunity that every generation had 83
8. The very land you walk on is alive 87
9. People in authority, who shift boundaries without permission, curse the land and the people who live on it 95
10. It's time to go back to the beaches and talk 101
11. God, what do you think about The Treaty of Waitangi? 107
12. You are bone of their bone, they are flesh of your flesh 115
13. If you want to know where next for Māori and Pākehā – listen to the cry of the land 123
14. Excuse me, God, but aren't we supposed to be talking about Māori and the sea? 127
15. Pākehā vs Māori: How did the accused come to be the judge and jury at this trial? 137
16. Māori Time – it's God's time 147
17. Māori and Pākehā. Your attitude toward each other wounds the land 157

18. So three guys, a Pākehā, a Māori and an Asian, all go to see God 165

19. Innocent blood cries out from your land, New Zealand...... 173

Special Bonus Book – What they never told you about how to have a back and forth conversation with God like a friend 181

How having a conversation with God healed our Marriage...... 185

The conversation with God that healed our Marriage 191

Six interviews with God about how to do this

1. Yes, you can hear God talk to you........ 199

2. You don't have to be perfect to hear him 207

3. How do you know it's really God? 213

4. What sort of question's can you ask him?........ 221

5. Is it always clear what God is saying? 227

6. What to do when you think God has broken a promise to you. . 235

How to have your own conversation with God

How to have a back and forth conversation with God........ 245

How to deal with Doubt........ 249

Does a conversation with God have to be in writing? 253

What can I have a conversation with God about? 255

Why isn't this common?........ 257

What to do if God doesn't seem to answer........ 259

What to do if God's answers sound too good? 261

How often can I have a conversation with God? 263

Why is there so much doubt and opposition?........ 265

What if I hear God wrong? 267

Why don't I have to be a better person first? 269

Why does God sound differently to each of us?........ 270

Is it difficult?........ 271

Important life lessons from the conversations

Life is a smorgasbord . . . 274
The better you choose to feel, the better you will feel . . . 275
If you pass kindness onto others, they will too . . . 276
A messy room is hardly life threatening . . . 277
Driving a Kenworth and a conversation with God . . . 278
Annette's Story . . . 280
Maggie's Story . . . 281
Ollie's Story . . . 282
Peacekeepers stay quiet . . . 283
Offence is more often taken . . . 285

The Bible and conversations with God

A few things we have learned about the conversations . . . 287
What does the Bible say about listening to God? . . . 291
Bible Heroes and Villains . . . 295
The Freedom Diaries . . . 299
The Freedom Assignment . . . 301
Mark and Miriam Speak to your Church or Group . . . 303

SPECIAL BONUS BOOK (PAGE 181)

"What They Never Told You About How To Have A Back And Forth Conversation With God"

Want to know how to have your own conversations with God about this subject?

Includes: Six amazing interviews with God about how to have your own conversation with him. Hear what God has to say to you about all this.

FOREWORD

BRADFORD HAAMI. MĀORI.
Author. Television Writer. Recognised Advisor on what God is saying about Māori, Pākehā and the Land. Expert on Māoritanga.

A white man who doesn't want to talk about the bloody history of his country, discovers to his horror that God does.

I thank Mark for being brave enough to publish this dangerous conversation. Having followed his God conversations with interest, I find *Cry the Wounded Land* not only refreshing but revealing. The notion of a 'Wounded Land' is a common phrase spoken in Māori circles, describing the painful dishonouring of Māori land tenure, bloodshed on the land, confiscation of territory, and the pillaging of its resources for colonial economic reasons. Land is an extremely pertinent subject; a key reason for on-going conflict between Māori and the Crown, and the underlying cause of suspicion and separation between Māori and Pākehā*.

In the 20 years of my personal time attending church (Pentecostal), I have seldom heard any sermon about the subject of land from any New Zealand pulpit. Is the issue of land too contentious or maybe even irrelevant in God's economy? Or is it considered as not important to New Zealand Gospel evangelists and preachers? As a Māori, a church goer and a past church elder, I find this extremely interesting. After being involved with a number of intercessory prayer team meetings and co-leading a British-Māori repentance journey through the historical land wars battle sites of New Zealand, land was a key subject continually raised by the Holy Spirit. Land, and how it is treated and mistreated, are strong issues on God's mind. He definitely wants to speak to us about land and people.

Indigenous lands and people have traditionally been lumped together under the concept of 'wilderness' by colonists, missionaries and settlers who sought to exploit and dominate them both for economic reasons.*

Taking dominion over the wilderness meant taking dominion over the people of the land as well. Exploitation of wilderness land for economic reasons was a settler ideal that turned out to be traumatic for Māori in so many ways.

Whenua means land and placenta in the Māori language; it is the place of nurturing and birth, life and fertility, as well as burial. Losing connection to land through dishonourable and unjust means has been painful for generations of Māori, and recent political apologies and compensations, whilst admirable, are inadequate for the deeper healing of hearts broken by past colonial actions. Some other revelation needs to come into this space.

I see how the Native American tribes have gathered to protest against the Dakota oil pipeline situation and I see that same determination and fortitude my own people have when it comes to land and injustice. There are so many voices speaking and proclaiming their views on these issues. There is the indigenous voice, and that of the colonists, Crown agents, corporate agents, legal beagles, journalists, academics. You name it, there are all types of words being expressed into the air about land.

But I wonder what the land itself is saying, even more importantly, what is God saying when he looks at humanity, the land and creation?

Romans 8:22 comes to mind; "The whole of creation has been moaning together as in the pains of childbirth until now". I believe the land and creation is moaning and speaking; waiting

**EDITOR'S NOTE: For those readers to whom Brad's comments may seem a little inflammatory, it seems worthwhile to point out that The Oxford Dictionary offers the following meanings for 'Colonise'; "Send settlers to (a place) and establish political control over it". "Settle among and establish control over (the indigenous people of an area)". "Appropriate (a place or domain) for one's own use."*

for God's plans on the earth, on the whenua of Aotearoa, to come into being. Not abortions or miscarriages but full term birth plans to be executed by the leading of His Spirit for the healing of pre-European and post-colonial iniquities against the land and the restoration of men and land.

Mark Holloway's *Cry the Wounded Land* is an apt conversation that will take the reader on a journey with the God of the Bible about His creation, His land, and His environment and our role, as humanity, in the full theatre of the greater picture. The conversations in this book are a timely, well-needed glimpse into God's blueprint for understanding how a deeper healing and relationship between land, people (Māori, Pākehā and tauiwi) and God could come about. This is a key. It transcends our own cultural, religious and secular insights on land, above it and under it. More than that, these conversations need faith to fully comprehend, and I thank Mark for being brave enough to publish this dangerous conversation. It is a dialogue he could not have concocted himself due to his limited knowledge on these indigenous/Māori issues - no offence, Mark.

Many will see this as fantastic or even mystic, but I'd have to say that much of what is penned here, the Holy Spirit has been imparting to many of us in our own prayer closets over the years. Seeds of this revelation He is planting into the hearts of men and into this whenua for the good of Aotearoa and abroad.

Mā Ngārangi-o-neherā koutou e whakapuaki ōna whakaaro hōhonu. May The Ancient of Days reveal his deeper thoughts to you all.

Nā Bradford Haami

Main book starts page 43

Foreword

David Garratt. Pākehā.

Songwriter. Co-founder Scripture and Song.

Respected Elder Statesman in International Christian circles.

Commentator on the relationship between Indigenous peoples, European settlers and the Land.

When I first read the conversations Mark had with God about Māori/Pākehā relationships, I was a little shocked.

God had been speaking to me for almost 30 years about this, and now the same subject, and especially about the land, was being revealed to a man who didn't even want to know about it!

However, as I began to think more about what Mark was hearing, I felt a deep satisfaction that God was revealing long hidden truths to him, even though he seemed a bit of a bull in a china shop. His sensitivity, and the way he would convey what God was impressing on him, was of course, just who he is.

Mark asked me for a Pākehā view point for *Cry the Wounded Land*. I have to say that these subjects have come to us at the right time and through an important channel.

The Holy Spirit first challenged me with my need to understand the culture of the Māori, as I was walking on a beach in 1987. It came out of the blue that I realised that the more than 20 albums Dale and I had produced, were all musically and lyrically a cultural expression that had nothing to do with the uniqueness of our own Indigenous people. It was out of ignorance that we never considered that the Māori had been given their own language and way to worship the Creator.

On that day I 'heard' two things. One was that in the future we would be seeing a new church, one where we wouldn't be led largely by a single European male leader but that cultural expressions and world views would be a part, and also that we would see cultural diversity in leadership. It was a prophetic word to me that I have waited all these years to see fulfilled.

I am still holding it in my heart.

The second thing I 'heard' was personal. It was that if I was to be of value to God in the days ahead, the same issues that God is giving Mark right now would continue to be a part of what I would pursue in the years ahead.

From my view point, the creator designed Māori and Pākehā to cohabit these Islands.

He gave us both unique giftings which, if offered in a spirit of humility, would see a nation where true unity in our diversity would be possible. For this to happen, however, we would both need to be flexible, in our cultural bents and respect the Spirit of God in each other. Even now this is very challenging. Past hurts, ignorance and arrogance have been the norm.

The fact is, God has invested unique aspects of His character in every Island and Continent on earth. As we realise this, and consider what Paul talks about in 1 Corinthians 12, we will realise that the example he used showing the diversity of the human body is truly the way the Creator works.

So "if the whole body was the eye, where would be the sense of hearing?" We both have important truths God has invested in us, but to really understand this, for me, required a genuine revelation.

When I was made aware of my need to learn from the Māori, the first thing God instructed me to do was 'listen'.

I had to realise that I had a bent to solve other people's problems even when they didn't ask me for help. I had to shut up and hear.

I'm still learning but at least I understand its importance. The thing is, I will never be Māori and Brad* will never be Pākehā. The body of Christ is not about conformity. Look at His creation, abundance and myriad variety – this is what He is all about.

The truths God is telling Mark concerning warfare are most important. We don't fight against flesh and blood – which so often has been, and still is, the case. The unity Jesus prayed for, learning to hear His Spirit, listening and laying aside our cultural bents, are keys to seeing His will done so that the land and her people can rejoice again.

One other interesting observation I see is that there is more interaction between Hawaiian and Māori people which will be a good thing as they learn from the strengths of each other.

Mark is on the right track, read and learn from him as he bares his heart in his own unique way.

David Garratt.

***EDITOR'S NOTE:** *Brad Haami is David's friend, and the author of the first forward to* Cry the Wounded Land.

Main book starts page 43

Why This Book?

Mark Holloway

I didn't get any warning that God wanted to talk about this.

One day, without any warning, I found myself in a back and forward conversation with God – about Māori and Pākehā. It took me completely by surprise. It wasn't what he and I had started out talking about that morning. When I realised where the conversation was going I tried to change the subject, but God kept bringing the discussion back to the brown and white story.

It's not only New Zealand that's bleeding.

When I published that first conversation, I got a lot of heartfelt response. Most of it was very positive, and it came from Māori and Pākehā. Many urged me to have more conversations like it. I even heard from people in other countries – South Africa, the USA, Canada, Australia, Ireland and others. They told me their nations are wounded too. It seems many of us need to move forward, as two or more people, on our different shared lands.

This topic is dangerous, there's been hurt on both sides, so I tried to change the subject, but God wouldn't let up.

I did my best to avoid the subject, but God kept starting new conversations about it. And each of those conversations drew intense interest from people I've never met.

Eventually he seemed to say that I should gather all those conversations together in one place to make it easier for people interested in this subject. So here they are – *Cry the Wounded Land* – conversations with God about Māori and Pākehā, and the Land.

WARRIOR NATION: This isn't my story, it's yours too – will you help me write the rest of it?

This book holds 19 of my conversations with God about our two mighty people, Māori and Pākehā, and New Zealand, our living, breathing land. If through my conversations with him, you hear his voice on the wind, then please start your own.

Prayer is powerful – but I'm asking you for something different.

By all means, pray for our land, it releases his power. But traditional prayer is not my subject, others are a lot better at that than me.

I'm asking you to do something different, to have your own back and forth conversation with God about this, just like you would with a friend. A conversation like Cain and Abraham, Moses and Balaam, Elijah, Jesus and Paul had. Yes they prayed and that released power, but they also had back and forth conversations with God that still tell us what he thinks about things.

It's time we had conversations like that too, about our two people and our land. Conversations so clear, that you can document them, and tell others, sentence by sentence, what he said to you. That's what I've done in this book. And now, I'm asking you to do it too. Will you help?

He wanted us, Māori and Pākehā, to show the world how to meld two great peoples together, a marriage, a powerful union.

If we don't get into a dialogue with him about this, one that we can share with others, he will have to wait another generation to show the world what he wanted to do through New Zealand.

I'm white, these are my conversations, but we need to hear God speak about this in brown voices, and white – yellow, black, red, and every other colour voice too. Please, please you warriors of the land, ask and document what he's saying. Tell us in words written down, tell us in words sung, stomped and shouted. Haka this to us, as we write and sing, and say it back to you. Kia Kaha (be strong).

Mark Holloway

PS: For readers from other countries; 'Pākehā' means European, Caucasian or white, New Zealander. 'Māori' are New Zealand's indigenous, or first nations people. 'Aotearoa' is the name the Māori gave this country before the Pākehā came. The 'Haka' is the war dance Māori are famous for right around the World.

SPECIAL BONUS BOOK

WANT TO KNOW HOW TO HAVE YOUR OWN CONVERSATIONS WITH GOD ABOUT THIS SUBJECT?

See back section of this book: Page 181

"What they never told you about how to have a back and forth conversation with God"

We invite you to read it, and then have your own back and forth conversations with God about Māori, Pākehā and this great land.

Mark & Miriam Holloway

Mark and Miriam live in Tauranga New Zealand, and have taught thousands of Kiwis, of all colours, to have their own back and forth conversations with God. Mark is the author of best seller *The Freedom Diaries.* In their other lives, Mark is an expert advisor to the business sector in the areas of marketing and sales – and Miriam drives big rig trucks.

Important Insights From Respected Others

Libby Huirua – Author, Songwriter 29
Winkey Pratney – Author, Bible Teacher 31
Norm McLeod – Author, Pastor 33
Josh Klinkenberg – Author, Songwriter 35
Jon McKenzie – Police Detective, Church Elder 37
Jackie Hawley – Gynaecologist 39

Main book starts page 43

When I was 19 I Heard God Speak

TO ME, PERSONALLY, FOR THE FIRST TIME

Libby Huirua. Author. Songwriter. Teacher.

I wasn't sure if I was allowed to have that level of relationship with Him. But something about it [hearing him speak like that] felt very right and normal, and I wanted to know Him more in that way, so I went with it!

My relationship with Him involved talking and listening, and the emotional intimacy that resulted from that relationship became the foundation for my life! I was so excited, nearly 30 years later, to be introduced to Mark's book *The Freedom Diaries*. I felt that same leap in my heart, reading about the depth of conversation that God wants to have with us, his kids, and the relationship that brings!

And now Mark has released this new book, *Cry the Wounded Land*. The conversations with God in this new book are precious and important insights into his heart for us as individuals, for our families, for our nation; for all nations!!

But woven throughout is simply the heart of God for the restoration of a conversational relationship with us – conversation that has the ability to heal, mould and change us. And in changing us, the world around us changes too!

Libby.

Main book starts page 43

God Gave The Māori People

Three great gifts

**Winkie Pratney. Author.
International Speaker and Teacher.**

This is a searching conversation at a significant time. Mark's unique talks with God in *The Freedom Diaries*, became for him a series of conversational exchanges well worth listening to. Even genuinely knowing the Lord, it is easy to forget we have this 'treasure in earthen vessels' and that "greater is He that is in us than he that is in the world" can bring the often unexpected, enlightening direction of the Holy Spirit to any serious seeking heart.

Cry the Wounded Land is an even more searching talk at an even more significant time. God gave to the Māori people who became the guardians for our nation (and to bless the other people-groups who followed) three great gifts for the unique treasure that is New Zealand; the calling for care and harvest of the Garden, the protection and defense of the Warrior, and the joy and creativity of the Entertainer. Despite the acknowledgement of 'How Great Thou Art' and our unequalled national anthem prayer of 'God Defend New Zealand', we all know what can happen if we lose what we were given and turn our gifts into arrogance. Take away what are signally His gifts of blessing and all you have left is an angry, drunk Māori who has lost it all in the river of no return. Get it back. Read the Book. Don't drop the ball. Start your own journal. Alternatives become unthinkable.

Winkie.

Main book starts page 43

Understanding

And even some solutions

Norm McLeod. Māori.
Founding pastor, House of Breakthrough.

Mark is a friend of mine; passionate in his love for God and people. He has genuine desire, and a gift that helps bring people into a deeper relationship with their creator.

His writings come to him as direct revelations. That's what makes *Cry the Wounded Land* so intriguing – he knows very little of our Māori history and doesn't pretend to have all the answers or solutions. Yet he's a genuine bloke, and a mate, and now he's using his gift to bring understanding, and maybe even some solutions to our wounded land.

Mark and I have talked about historic injustices to Māori and the Church's role to help bring healing. He does not pretend to be an expert on any of these matters, in fact he openly admits he's just a Pākehā boy who knows very little.

I am amazed at the number of New Zealanders, especially Christians, who know so little, sometimes nothing, about our indigenous history between God, the Church, the Crown and the settler Church.

Cry the Wounded Land is not intended to bring a guilt trip about the past. But it will bring understanding of where we are today as Māori in society and how that's come about. And it may help to reveal to our beautiful Pākehā Whānau, the perspective that some of us Māori have, of the predominantly Pākehā style of Church in Aotearoa today.

Norm.

Main book starts page 43

The Sound Of the Land

HAS BEEN TALKED ABOUT FOR YEARS

Josh Klinkenberg. Songwriter. Author. Teacher.

When I first heard 'those words' said, something inside me resonated – I loved what I heard! But I still had no idea what it meant. Then as we began to journey with indigenous cultures, especially our amazing Māori people here in New Zealand, we began to find the answers to the questions that we had.

We see many scriptures talking about the sound and song of the land, but often times we view these through European lenses and take them to simply be 'nice metaphors.' What if they weren't?

We have learnt so much from being accepted and welcomed into Māori culture. What a gift it is to be included as one of their own! In this journey, one of the life changing keys we have discovered is the connection we are destined to share with the land.

It really hit home for me when I was on a trip to the USA a number of years ago. We were sitting in a recording studio wearing sweatshirts, jackets, jeans, and anything warm we could find. The odd thing about this was, it was the middle of their summer and it was 45 degrees outside!!!

It was in that time that the Lord began to teach us a valuable lesson that would forever change us...

One of the many differences between western and indigenous cultures is that western culture often changes the world around it, to suit its own wants and needs; whereas indigenous culture will fit in with its surroundings and adapt to the environment. Both cultures have strengths (and weaknesses) which benefit the other, but this one realisation opened our eyes to so much when it came to the concept of hearing 'the sound of the land.'

When our European ancestors, the colonisers, came to these shores, they came with their own sound. A dominant sound. A sound that had a goal of being heard louder than any other sound. This isn't always a bad thing, and it has some great kingdom strengths to it. But when the Māori came to these shores, they came with a different heart all together.

Māori did not come with their own sound, but rather with a heart to hear and discover the song that was already being sung. They came with a heart to listen and participate in the song that creation was singing. We see it in the Māori instruments and how they imitate the sounds of our native bush and surroundings. We see it in the connection and love that Māori share for the land itself. It has been our joy to fall in love with both Māori and the land on which we now live.

I am excited about the pages of this book being read throughout our beautiful little nation as I believe it will stir an awareness and value for the song the land is singing. May we all discover the joy of falling in love with each other and with the very land we walk on. As it reads in the pages of this book, the very land is alive and we have an opportunity which will change the course of history for generations to come!

Josh.

Main book starts page 43

What's On God's Heart

FOR THE VERY DIRT WE STAND ON?

Jon McKenzie. Police Detective and Church Elder.

I love this book, it's a book of healing. Actually, it's less of a book, and more of a conversation with God about our country, Aotearoa (New Zealand). To me that's significant, and I suspect it is for many others... to read what's on God's heart for us, for the very dirt we stand on, and the people we walk amongst. And then there's the other thing I like; this book is not just about healing, but about purpose and destiny, what God wants for Aotearoa and all who inhabit her. This book is an invitation from God to reconnect back into the original path that He has called us to walk together. This is a book of hope and revelation, not accusation and judgement.

I'm a police officer. I've worked at the coal face, policing New Zealand's deepest darkest secrets and social problems for the last 28 years. I've observed the pain that exists in our nation. The dream of 'Godzone' (God's own) is a long way from the reality. Many in church never get to see what is happening out there. Sadly I have come to see the total ineffectiveness, how disconnected the church and most Christians are from the pain that walks around us every day in this land. It has also become obvious that so many of the issues I deal with bubble up from the hurt and pain sown into the land over the past 200 years. 200 years of colonisation and robbing Māori of their land, culture and identity. This is just the sad truth of 28 years working amongst the pain, disillusionment, loss and anger of many Māori.

And then there's *Cry the Wounded Land*. I believe this book is a significant insight into what God is saying about all this. These conversations with God make sense to things I see daily and have pondered over many years. They give insight into what we are facing on this collective journey as Kiwis. But more than a commentary on the problem, it provides solutions....God solutions. I love reading the heart of Jesus for our nation, and the challenge to take part in bringing healing, rather than just leaving it to someone else to fix. It is time for each one of us to become a part of the journey to heal our land. This is a significant and timely book for our nation.

If you care about Aotearoa, then this book is a worthwhile investment. But be warned, it has the potential to strip you down, challenge you and make you look very deep into yourself and what you believe, about yourself and our nation. I invite you on this journey because we are in a time to bring about the healing that God always intended for us, as brothers, Māori and Pākehā, to walk together into the destiny God planned for us.

Oh, and finally; in these conversations, God calls for action. It's time to start picking the right fight; not against each other, Māori and Pākehā, but against our true enemy – the devil. I believe this book is an imperative for every Kiwi. To quote God from these pages, "If you look back with honesty then you can look forward in a way that heals, together." Why? Because God declares that He could see that we would be better together, Māori and Pākehā.... Awesome!!!! This book is about healing our land. For us, our kids and the generations to come. It's too big to ignore and just leave for someone else to sort. Read and be inspired to start your own conversation with God on these issues, so that together we can find our way forward into our healing and destiny (take my word for it....we desperately need it).

Jon.

Main book starts page 43

This Book Challenges

FOUNDATIONAL BELIEFS

Jackie Hawley. Gynaecologist, Pākehā and Devout Aotearoean.

This book makes uncomfortable reading. It's not kosher. It is difficult to digest. It is deeply disturbing on so many levels. It is also uniquely beautiful, and in parts quite divine. Mark, in all his 'Mark-ness' – amidst his brashness, white, Pākehā maleness, vulnerably presents his innermost banter. This honest vulnerability is remarkable. As such, I trust it will not be trampled upon, but will be treated with the kind respect it deserves.

I can confirm to the reader, that this 'dialogue' is genuine. It is written the same way Mark talks. He continues with the discipline introduced in his first book – that of taking time to spend 'in conversation' with the inner voice, diarising as he goes.

Mark is a noticer, reflective, remembers detail and is able to listen well. For all his strong personality and opinions, he is very open to new concepts and expanding theology. Mark and his wife Miriam are actively engaging with the Māori communities across New Zealand. This writing is birthed from times of solitude, reflection and prayer, and a heart for this land and her people. Mark has mastered the ability to capture and surface deeper thoughts.

In my view, this book is masterfully clever. The paragraphs attributed to The Creator, God, the Māori call him 'Io', are refreshingly divine. Surprises abound. The 'God bits' are friendly, have unexpected grace notes and openness, are frank but non-judging, and respectful of Mark's limitations and boundaries, express empathy, and present a very 'big picture' perspective. The God of these conversations is a pursuer of justice and relationship (not repentance), and is speaking out hopes for

Healing of our Land and our Peoples. This God is quite safe to approach, to listen to, to question and to challenge – likeable and awesome.

This book resonates with truth and weaves hope. It also succinctly challenges foundational beliefs on just about everything – who we are, the Nature of God, New Zealand history, status, the Pākehā view of things, God's relationship with us, and our relationship with God. It suggests not only that we can learn from nature, but that the ground itself might speak and echo the human heart!

The questions are: How seriously ought we take the scripts attributed to the Creator ? Is our land, Aotearoa, truly 'wounded'? If so, how do we individually and corporately respond?

Threaded gently amongst the uncomfortable stuff there is a call to deep and Holy listening between peoples of this land, and between the People and Nature (the land).

Are we willing to deeply listen to the divine within and amongst us? This listening may be just what is needed, now, for Māori and Pākehā together, to bring healing to our nation and navigate the optimal way forward for our children and this place – God's zone.

Wishing you Good Reading.

Jackie.

Main book starts page 43

Cry the Wounded Land

Conversations with God about Māori, Pākehā and the Land

MARK HOLLOWAY

Cry The Wounded Land

I wanted your people to walk gently when they came to this land. But they didn't

God, the other night I was driving and I made a big mistake – I asked what you wanted to say. And right out of the blue you said 'Mark, walk gently on the land'.

Yes. Is there a problem?

Yes, there is! You know there is!! That's an indigenous sort of thing to say and I'm white. I had absolutely no idea what you were talking about and then I arrive at that meeting in Kawerau and David Garratt's talking all about the land.

So what's wrong with that?

God, if David hadn't been talking about it I might have been able to forget that you said it, pretend that you hadn't.

Why would you want to? I don't want you to forget it, Mark.

But I do, God! It's too deep and I don't know enough about it.

You asked me what I wanted to talk about. This morning I want to talk about the land. Is that OK?

No, it's not OK God! The subject's too big, too dangerous. You don't

read much about it in the Bible.

Yes you do.

Really?

Really.

Well God, if no one else was listening then it wouldn't be so bad! I mean I'd still be out of my depth, I know nothing about spiritual matters surrounding the land, but if you insist on talking about it, then why not do it in private?? That way I could learn what you were saying without annoying anyone else.

Why is it important what others think?

Because this is going to polarise people's thinking, God. And that's crazy because I don't even know which side I'm on. I'm white and I don't understand the issues. And it's not a subject I want to divide people's thinking on. It's not my subject. My subject is setting people free from Religion.

How?

By having a back and forward conversation with you.

Exactly – this is a back and forward conversation, Mark.

God, you're impossible!! Anyway, talking about a conversation with you gets me in enough political trouble without having to start talking about the whole white/indigenous 'Pākehā/Māori' thing. It's too big, God. It's huge in just about every colonised country. And what do I know about it?? Nothing at all!!

I want to teach you about it.

Really?? I'm ignorant about this God, and I think I'd like to stay that way. I'd like to stay out of this if I could – the implications are just

waaay too big. I've read a little bit of the history and I realise it's nothing like what we got taught at school. I'll admit I am horrified at some of the stuff we did, but I'm white, so I have plenty of reasons to think that maybe it wasn't so bad. As I said, the subject's just too big.

So you want to sit on the fence?

Well no, but there's no point making myself unpopular talking about something I don't have a strong viewpoint over. I just know that it's a big can of worms I'd rather not open. Getting caught in crossfire when you're not involved is silly. The wounds are too deep, God.

You're involved, Mark. I want you to explain the historical accounts you're talking about.

No!! Not really God? Not here?

Why not?

Because they're stories that demand answers and I don't have any.

I do though.

You mean Orakau?

I mean Orakau.

OK, one day I was driving along and needed a cup of tea so I pulled over at one of those roadside picnic areas and there was a monument there. So I took my cup of tea over and read the monument, as you do.

What did it say? This bit is important.

Well, on one side it said 'Rewi Maniapoto', that's all. Just that name. But on the other side it said all about how the British forces under Cameron had fought a great battle there.

And?

Well, it seemed a bit weird. I wondered who Rewi Maniapoto was and how come only his name was on the monument and yet the British got a big story. It seemed a bit one-sided somehow. So I grabbed my phone and googled the name of the battle site – Orakau.

And?

And it wasn't a pretty story.

Tell the story.

Come on, God!! Ladies read this.

It's a story about ladies, Mark. The land has cried for ladies and when ladies cry for the land the healing will begin.

See what I mean, God! It's too deep. I don't know if you really just said that. What if I got the whole Māori protocol thing wrong right there. Are women even meant to cry for the land?

Everyone is meant to cry for the land – just as the land cries for everyone. Tell the story, Mark.

Alright, well the bit that got me was that a few days after the British surrounded the Pa at Orakau, the Māori, including a lot of women and children, left the Pa. They didn't come out and attack the British, they just left.

And?

And the next bit disgusted me, God. Made me ashamed to be white. I wondered how come we don't get taught this stuff at school??

Who writes the textbooks, Mark?

There you go again, God! That's why I don't want to be involved in this discussion, it's highly provocative and you just make it worse.

Tell the story, Mark.

OK, the British, instead of letting them go, pursued them with a hail of bullets. And then they chased and bayoneted them, including the women as they lay wounded. At least 160 of the pā's occupants were killed. Interpreter William Mair expressed his 'disgust at the generally obscene and profane behaviour of the troops'.

But that's not the whole story, Mark.

OK. Well, at the end it said that once they'd finished killing, the British then set their sights for Tauranga.

And why did that make you so mad??

Because I know what happened next. When they got to Tauranga the church missionary Archdeacon Brown, invited the senior officers for dinner. I mean, God, what on earth would the Māori have thought?? The British slaughter their women and children, and then as if to celebrate, the leader of the church in Tauranga invites them around for dinner!

Does that sound like the revelation of the sons of God that the land is waiting for, Mark?

You don't even need to ask, God. It wasn't just the government and the army involved in the slaughter of women and children – but the church was involved too. If I was a Māori, I would have cursed the church and commanded my descendants never to set foot in it.

Yes, but the Māori didn't did they?

No. That's what makes the story even worse somehow.

Why?

Because the Māori chief in Tauranga, I can't remember his name...

Look up his name. Names should never be forgotten. The land remembers the names. The land holds the innocent and the guilty for a future time.

Oh man, God. I'm going to get in trouble for that, and I have no way of defending myself – I don't even understand what you just said.

What was the Tauranga chief's name, Mark?

It says he was the Ngai Te Rangi Chief, Rawiri Puhirake.

What did Rawiri do that impressed you, Mark?

It embarrasses as much as it impresses me! He showed us up badly! He acted more Christian than the British. He suggested to Cameron that they both agree to a strict 'rules of conduct of battle', and they were biblical rules – all straight out of the Bible. And the sad, sad thing is that the Māori who learned those biblical rules from the British obeyed them, but the British largely ignored them.

So what are you thinking, Mark?

God, there are still cultural differences. Still things that make me uncomfortable about Māori, things I don't understand. But if I allow myself to think about stories like this one, I won't be able to hide behind cultural discomfort. We were the tyrants, the murderers of women and children, the liars and the cheats. We were the savages!! It's hard to get the words out, God. Surely we should let the past be the past?

Yes, when it is past.

What's that supposed to mean?

You need to go back to the beginning and learn what you were meant to learn back then.

Is this more about repentance?

No. This is different. Repentance is not the original reason I called your people to this land. I want you to go back to the beginning to learn why you were brought here. What you were meant to learn. You thought you came here of your own design, but actually you were called here by me. But you never knew that because you didn't know how to listen. And that's still the problem for most.

Really? What were we meant to learn?

To walk gently on the land. But instead you came and trampled all over it, killing its inhabitants in order to steal their land.

They killed us too, God. They weren't innocent.

Mark, I'll talk to them about what they did. But right now I'm talking to you about what you did.

I want you to talk about the next part of the Tauranga war and then we'll finish with the key point of this discussion – which is that you all need to walk gently on the land – and why that's so important.

OK well, I'm a bit rusty on this bit but what I do know has always troubled me, and that's probably bad because I don't know all the details. But after the battle of Gate Pa, a few weeks later, Colonel Greer was riding along with 600 men I think, and he saw that the Māori were building a new pā. These were Māori who were still observing strict rules of conduct, erecting another arena for battle and would then have invited the British to come and have another fair fight.

Yes?

When Greer rode past with his 600 men, he realised his opportunity to surprise the Māori, so he turned back and charged and slaughtered them. It's embarrassing to be white when I read something like that God... but the worst thing is that somehow his cowardly act got commemorated as heroic.

How?

We, the whites, decided to name a large and important part of Tauranga after him. We called it Greerton.

Mark, when you call the land names that commemorate cowardly slaughter, you do great harm.

Are you talking specifically about Greerton?

No, not specifically. The blood of those you slay causes the land great pain. I want to talk about what I called you here for.

What did you call us here for?

To listen to me in a new place. When you first arrived you should have asked me what I was saying. Then, you should have walked gently on to the land, and asked those here before you what I had said to them before you got here. If you had known how to have a conversation with me, you would have heard me say all that. You would have walked onto this land as a guest. A guest, not a conqueror. You would have heard me say what I said to Paul in Athens – that I was already speaking to this people.

But no, that would have been too humbling for you. That would have been to admit that these mere 'savages' as you called them, might have heard something from me before you came. And they did. All men do. All men hear from me, Mark. Some knowingly, some unknowingly. Paul told you that.

> *"Because that which is known about God is evident within them; for God made it evident to them. For since the creation of the world His invisible attributes, His eternal power and divine nature, have been clearly seen, being understood through what has been made."* *ROM 1:19-20*

Māori understand this better than you. The people of the land always do. I wanted you to learn that from them. But instead of allowing them to teach you what I had already been saying here, you demanded that they listen to you talk about what I had been saying where you had come from.

Oh man God, this is waaaay too big.

No.

What should we do then?

Walk gently on the land, ask them what I have been saying.

What if they don't know anymore?

Ask them to ask me. I will remind them. And I will tell them what I am saying now.

The plan was very simple, Mark. I had been saying things on and to this land before you arrived. I called you here to hear those things. My plan was that you would ask them what I had been saying and they would teach you. And then they, intrigued by your humility, would have asked what you had been hearing where you came from. It was to be an example to the world of how to meld two cultures. But it still hasn't happened.

Both sides are implicated in this. Both sides have faults. This isn't about blame or even repentance. I want to wind the clock back to what should have happened. I want to rewind this whole scenario back to the beginning, back to when you first arrived, so that you can do what should have happened then.

You need this, the land needs this. This is about what should have happened back then but didn't. The land is cursed when you curse it with blood. That's what David Garratt was telling you. But none of you really understand what it means. Neither side does. You need to ask me. But first you must come walking gently on to the land. You came after them. Ask them what I was saying before you got here. Doing so restores to them the responsibility to hear me.

I want them to hear me, not blame you. I want them to teach you what they hear from me. That's how I wanted it to start and together you would have painted a clearer picture of me in this place. There's still time. But not much. The repentance is good but it's not the actual purpose I called the two peoples together for.

Does that mean they should be the bosses?

Nobody should be the bosses. This was to be the melding of two peoples. Each learning from the other. But you wanted to do all the teaching. That never works, Mark. Never. First you needed to listen. Because you were the guests, it was your place to listen first – the conqueror comes shouting, the guest comes listening. If you had listened, they would have too.

I wish I'd never heard all this, God.

Yes, quite. I've been saying this since you first arrived, Mark, and I'll keep saying it until someone listens. As you rightly pointed out, the church wasn't listening back then, do you think they're listening now?

God, I'm not even going to answer that.

That's certainly the safest option, Mark.

When You Destroy Their Culture, You Also Destroy Your Own

When you systematically take away what another person is like, you lose as much as they do

God, I think I just heard you say that I should listen to what you say through the trees and the wind and the rain??

You did.

God, are you sure?? That sounds so indigenous, or ethnic somehow – sort of American Indian, or maybe Māori.

What's wrong with that?

I'm not ethnic or indigenous, God! I'm a white boy, out of my depth on this.

Yes, you are.

Good. I'm glad we're agreed on that, God. It sounds like something I'd expect to hear in a book about tribal wisdom??

Yes.

OK, you'd better explain a bit.

There's a lot to explain. The thing is that you have so much to learn from each other. Other people groups bring new knowledge to you. They bring discomfort because of cultural differences, but they bring new knowledge too. And you need their knowledge. You need theirs, they need yours. If they remove your culture they do you harm, and if you remove theirs you do them harm.

OK... so what are you saying here, God? This conversation has taken a very unexpected turn. I'm completely out of my depth now. This is a political hot potato and I'd rather not be holding on to it. We started out talking about listening to you.

We still are, Mark. The emphasis in this discussion, and remember there are many discussions you need to have with me about mixing people groups – conversations about what has happened in your history, conversations about what's happening right now, and conversations about what has yet to happen – but the emphasis in this particular discussion is not the harm that each group does to the other.

Right now I want to talk about the harm you do to yourselves when you remove another people's culture.

God, that's a dangerous thing to say. It sounds like I'm taking a side and I don't know enough about this to know which side to take. Actually, God, it sounds like you're taking a side!

I never take sides, Mark. I am never on a side. But I almost always favour the oppressed, so both sides would do well to make sure they never take the role of the oppressor.

I want you to understand that when you systematically take away another people's culture you lose just as much as they do. You lose the things in their culture which I intended you to gain. You would have gained those things had you asked me how to dance the delicate dance of melding two cultures into one. Melding cultures requires that both cultures are maintained as you join them to make something even better. When one culture is dominated and removed by the other, it harms both cultures.

Instead of demanding that they learn your religion, you should have asked me what I wanted you to learn from theirs. Every people group has truth they have received direct from me – some knowingly, some without realising it.

This is getting dangerous, God!!

Listen, Mark:

> *"So Paul, standing before the council, addressed them as follows: "Men of Athens, I notice that you are very religious in every way, for as I was walking along I saw your many shrines. And one of your altars had this inscription on it: 'To an Unknown God.' This God, whom you worship without knowing, is the one I'm telling you about..."* *ACTS 17:22-23*

So, God, I'm thinking here about 'EOI'...? I think that's how the Māori described you, 'the one God', didn't they have that concept before we ever turned up? I think they did. I think that's what they called you?

Google it, Mark.

OK I did – Google says the Māori recognised there was a supreme being called 'Io'.

Yes, they did. They owned some of the truth before you got here – and you owned some truth too before you arrived. Think about it. I had spoken to them and they had heard that truth right here in New Zealand before you ever turned up. Imagine if you had asked what they had discovered about 'Io', imagine if you had learned from them, and they from you and together you had been able to paint a clearer picture of me and what I look like in this land. Imagine that!

If you had learned their truths from them, you would be able to live more natural lives, you would be able to count your blessings more easily and hear me with less effort.

Really, God??

Yes. You say of the indigenous cultures that they are 'more spiritual'. And you're right, they are. That was something I intended should be added to your culture. It's not too late. And if you learn from them, they can then learn from you. My agenda, not yours. You both have things to teach the other. Then together, both of your cultures will more readily embrace third cultures, and fourth and fifth. Each culture adding to and learning from the other. Not dominating but learning from. There are more cultures here already and more still coming, Mark. You need to learn this lesson that each new culture brings new truth to add.

Why tell me, God?

Because if you had learned from them how to hear me speak in the trees, the wind and the rain, it would have seen you strive less. I want you all to strive less. I want you simply to let me talk rather than think you have to strive to be good enough to hear me.

WANT TO KNOW HOW TO HAVE YOUR OWN CONVERSATIONS WITH GOD ABOUT THIS SUBJECT?

See back section of this book: Page 181

"What they never told you about how to have a back and forth conversation with God"

A Wild And Fierce Band Of Brothers

I brought Māori and Pākehā together to fight a common enemy, not to fight each other

Mark, your enemy is afraid of Māori and Pākehā together, so he has kept you apart because when two brothers fight against a common foe, first one brother leads, and then the other – and so on. Respect and might carry them in the battle.

Mark, everyone knows that Māori and Pākehā fighting together are an indomitable force, feared by many armies down through history – but the reason I drew you together was to fight an invisible army.

God, why do you insist on talking about these things?? I know nothing at all about them.

That's the nature of a conversation with me, Mark. When you learn to hear me speak about the little things, you'll hear big things too. Things you know nothing about.

OK, well I'm not sure I want to hear these 'big' things, God. They're too big. You're talking about crazy things like the haka, the sound of the wild spaces, and the didgeridoo. I'm going to be labelled 'fringe' for these discussions. People will say I've 'gone ethnic'.

You have gone 'ethnic', Mark! You all have. The moment your people set foot on this land you 'went ethnic'.

God, do you have to talk like this?

Mark, it needs to be said. It needs to be blown on the Māori war trumpet and the Pākehā bugle. Your enemy needs to be put on notice that a new people is beginning to stand up.

'Māori war trumpet'? Is there even such a thing, God??

Look it up, Mark.

OK, I did, and Wikipedia talks about Pūkāea and Pūtātara.

Yes, that'll do, but there are others. Māori know the correct names and there are sacred names too. This subject needs to be announced, to the land and to your enemy. It's well overdue. The land trembles with anticipation for it. And no, I'm not talking about the earthquake, Mark, it's much deeper than that! It's the reason you Pākehā want to rise up, shout and stamp when you hear the haka. It's why Kiwis of all colours love the stories of the Māori Battalion and their bravery, the way other armies were terrified of them in the World Wars. When you're on the same side, you Pākehā and Māori are dangerous – wild and dangerous!! I knew you would be before you ever set eyes on each other. It's why I called you together. There is a spiritual battle to fight and my plan was that you fight it together.

I didn't bring you here to fight the Māori, and I didn't put them here to fight you. I wanted you to fight alongside each other against a number of invisible enemies. Unseen armies that already warred against both of your peoples. You need Māori to help you fight the demonic forces that already warred with you before you came.

They need you Pākehā to help war against their own demonic enemies. But instead, you have been fooled into fighting each other. It takes your combined attention off your common enemy. His strategy is divide and conquer, and he has achieved it well with the two of you. He is afraid of you together, so he has kept you apart.

God, I worry that my Pākehā friends will think I've 'gone Māori' and that my Māori friends will think I don't know what I'm talking about (and I don't!)

Mark, don't worry about what others think. You haven't gone 'all Māori', you're still as white as the day you were born. These issues we're discussing are neither Māori nor Pākehā, they're Kiwi. I'm not asking you to be a Māori. And I don't want the Māori to be Pākehā. That's the whole issue. You tried to make them Pākehā, but it doesn't work for them. And neither will it work for you to try to be Māori. You can learn and borrow the best from each other's culture but you need to retain the strength of your own. They need you to do that. You need them to do that.

I think I can hear you saying this is important in any relationship?

Of course! Whether it's a relationship between two cultures or two people, the principles are the same. One must not smother the other. Neither must one try to become the other. Each does best by learning the other's strengths without losing their own. That's what gives a relationship strength.

So where are we going with this, God?

I'm talking about why I brought your two cultures together. It was my plan. My Spirit called your people here. Not because the Māori needed you, but because you both needed each other. It's the same in any great relationship, it works best when you both need each other equally. And you do.

That's what this was supposed to be about, each culture building the other up, but instead one dominated the other. And make no mistake, they would have dominated you even more effectively if the numbers were in their favour. Your people are warlike, but theirs even more so. And that is one of the things I wanted you to learn from them – their wonderful warlike strength. But instead you stole their land, smothered their language and squashed their spirit. Yes, they would have done the same to you had they been able. And that's my point. I brought you together to fight, but instead you fight each other.

You fight alongside each other in sport and war, but at home you are not ready to fight together against the invisible armies that war against you. You leave yourselves wide open because you operate as two peoples, each suspicious of the other. But my plan was that you would be two separate and unique peoples fighting as one.

Part of the invisible army that wars against you was here already shadowing the Māori – and part of it came here shadowing you.

Is this like the story that Graham Turner told me in Ohope?

Yes, exactly. Graham has part of this story. So does Brad Haami. So do many, many others. I have given parts of this story to many people, a lot of them don't fit the status quo, but they carry the story nonetheless. The more you share it, the more you will discover. Tina's dad told her the story of Orakau and his dad told him. The healing has begun, but as Tina told you, the hurting (mamae) is still there. And Mark, the land still holds that hurt. So many stories, Mark – some white, some brown. No one has the whole picture. When two brothers join forces to fight a common enemy, first one leads, then the other, and so on.

That's what this country was meant to look like. I brought you here as a gift to Māori, and I had them here ready as a gift for you – but neither of you looks anything like a gift. You have brought wonderful benefits but at huge cost, far too great a cost. I wanted you to share their country with them, and they would have shared it with you if you had come open handed, but you tore the country from their hands and mine.

This sounds very one-sided, God!! What about the stuff they did?

Mark, I will talk to them about what they did. And there is much to talk about. Far more than you can imagine. But my focus isn't just on repentance.

Good one, God!! I just lost half my readers right there. Us Christians are convinced that you are focused on us repenting and you forgiving.

Yes, there is a great deal of confusion surrounding that. Of course repentance is extremely important, but it must not rise above its appointed place! Repentance is a solution to the problems that occur on a journey – but is not the journey itself.

I didn't put you on earth to repent, I put you here to create. When mistakes are made, repentance is sometimes required, but it's not the end game, not what you're actually here for.

Mark, the journey is what I am focused on. The things that each of you, Māori and Pākehā understand about the other, I wanted you to bring to the unseen journey. Each of you gives lip service to the things that the other brings to the journey – Pākehā acknowledge the Māori love of the journey itself – Māori acknowledge the way you Pākehā focus on the final destination. But neither of you learn from the other's focus in any great depth. You're too busy pushing the other away or repenting for pushing them away.

It's time to learn and move on together. A wild and dangerous band of brothers!

And sisters, God?

Of course and sisters!! Without the sisters, you cannot even hope to fight. Of course there is more repenting to do, there often is when you put a relationship back together. Just when you think it's all wonderful, you come across old wounds that need addressing, but there is a time when the main focus needs to be going on together, not saying sorry for the past. That time is here.

It is time to work out how you will move forward together.

There's a battle coming at you in the hidden realms, you need to be preparing to fight it.

What about the people who are doing the repenting?

That's good. That's their job. They know it, and are doing it. But it's also time to focus on the reason I called you together, time to prepare for war.

How on earth do we prepare, God?

You learn from the other, you teach each other your individual arts of spiritual warfare. And you practise the fight – together. You're in for a fight, Mark, in for a pounding, but I have plans for you to stand your ground – two peoples standing as one army. To fight like there's no tomorrow with the courage that Māori bring to the fight, and to fight a planned fight the way you Pākehā do.

Mark, stand still and listen to this:

I am looking for the combined fierceness of the two people, melded together like a spear thrown with great might and striking home at your enemy.

A Story Of Two People With Blood On Their Hands

A story that's a 'little bit' brown and a 'little bit' white – And why I don't like the word 'Colonists'

Excuse me, God, but have you noticed that I'm white?

Yes, actually. I noticed before you were born. I noticed before the foundation of the world. I always knew you'd be white.

OK, then why tell me all these 'brown things' that you're telling me. I'm not equipped to understand them.

Oh really?

What's that supposed to mean, God?

What makes you say that the things we're discussing are 'brown things'?

Well, they are, God! They're all about Māori, the land and the way we should be working together.

Who's we, Mark?

Māori and Pākehā.

And which are you?

Pākehā, that's what I'm trying to say God, I'm white.

Māori and Pākehā did you say, Mark?

Yes!! Māori and Pākehā - man you can be frustrating God!

So… Māori and Pākehā… so we're not actually talking 'brown things', we're talking 'brown and white things'.

OK yes, I guess so. What's your point, God? (I can't actually believe I'm talking to you like this. That you really want to talk to me about this stuff and you put up with me, actually invite me to vent my frustration at you.)

I've put up with a lot worse than that in my time, Mark, carry on.

No you carry on, God, I want to stay out of this, you're the one making a point. I have a horrible feeling I know what it is, but I'd rather you came right out and said it.

Alright. You could have made the point for me. You can hear me in your heart quite clearly before it moves up to your mind and forms into clear words that you can write down. The point I'm making, Mark, is that these things we're discussing aren't 'brown things' as you put it. They are brown and white things. A little bit brown and a little bit white. And you're white, which is a full half of the story.

I need to explain this to brown and white. If I explained it to just one of you, then that would destroy the message. The message is that you need each other. If I only told this story to one of you, the other would assume that I favoured the one I told. But I don't.

You don't what?

I don't favour either of you.

You could have fooled me, God! It sounds like it's all our fault – it

sounds like we're the bad guys and they're the good guys.

Listen a little more carefully, Mark, that's not what I'm saying. I'm telling this story to you both. I'm telling this story to brown and white, because these things are brown and they are white.

You're saying something else behind that aren't you?

Actually, yes. You know what you've been taught about business partnerships?

You mean the idea that the only way to make a partnership work is if each partner does 90% of the work?

Yes. And this is a business partnership, Mark. A brown and white partnership and you've got a lot of business to catch up on. You have a country that needs to be husbanded and cared for.

Why do you keep saying the word 'brown' before you say the word 'white'?

When I'm talking to them, it's the other way around.

Why?

Because I want a partnership between your two peoples.

God, have you noticed that it's not just us two anymore? There are Chinese, Pacific Islanders, Indians and many new European, Asian and Arabic nations joining us.

Yes, there is a plan for you and all of those people in partnership too. A plan that will flow more easily if we can tidy up and get the original partnership working first. It's overdue, Mark. If that partnership had been working in the first place, you would have welcomed new nation after new nation in a completely different way. This nation was meant to look a lot different than it does.

OK; you were talking about 'a little bit brown and a little bit white'?

Actually, the description 'little bit' was just a poetic way to state the case, but the truth is much bigger than that, Mark. It's not really a 'little bit' at all.

Pardon?

Mark, the truth is that the topics you and I are discussing....

I'm not discussing those topics, you just keep opening them up and dropping them on me when you know I'm way out of my depth.

No you're not. You're white and these are brown and white topics – actually they're a big bit brown and a big bit white. These topics involve both of you, brown and white, to a very large extent and guess what, Mark? You're white!

You're not out of your depth here at all, not any more than your brown friends. You've got half the story and they've got half. Actually you've got the whole story and they've got the whole story too. This is all about you and... all about them too. This partnership won't work unless both sides take 90% or more of the responsibility to move forward.

Are you beginning to get this, Mark? This is big. Very big. And don't panic, it's not just you I'm saying it to. So listen up. You know all about this, you're not out of your depth in any way. And they know all about this too, and they're not out of their depth in any way either. This is your combined story – brown and white – this is your story together.

God, I feel a bit like one of two brothers getting a telling off by Dad.

You are one of two brothers, and I am talking to you both. But this is not a telling off. I am not the one who accuses brothers - I have to listen to his diatribe, but you don't. So don't! I'm not telling you off,

I am talking to you both. I'm saying 'hey guys, hey brown and white, how about you each take on 90% of the responsibility to sort this mess out?'

How about you both make this story a big bit brown and a big bit white? How about it?? Because if you do, you'll terrify your enemy and drive him backwards. You'll show him that all the mess he's made and the strongholds he's built in the last 200 plus years can be ripped open in a moment of time – and you'll show the world how it's done too. You were supposed to show the world how it's done right from the start of the Aotearoa story – the colonising nations needed to see an example. They needed to see that I didn't want them to colonise.

God, when you said the word 'colonise' just then, I realised I didn't even really know what it means. I mean, I've always thought of it as a nice British settler sort of word – it sounds quaint, and 'early days' or something.

And?

And so I thought I'd better look it up to see what it really means.

And?

I wish I hadn't, God!! Clearly we've sugar-coated the word because I never realised it meant these things. It's a sinister word!! Why did we even bother with a Treaty God? We obviously didn't have any sort of Treaty in mind if our plan was to 'colonise'.

Explain what the word 'colonise' means, Mark.

OK God, I just looked it up and the dictionary gives three definitions;

"To send settlers to (a place) and establish political CONTROL over it."

"To settle among and establish CONTROL over (the indigenous people of an area)."

"To APPROPRIATE (a place or domain) for one's use."

What are you thinking?

I'm thinking I wish I hadn't asked for this discussion.

You didn't, I did. That's the nature of a conversing God, Mark. I raise topics for discussion too. The way so many of you see me, the God you come and make requests to, that sort of God is bound by the topics you want to talk about. The best I can do in those sorts of situations is give you a nudge or an impression about a topic, and if you pick up on it, you begin to pray about it. In a conversation, it's different. I am able to frequently and often suggest topics. I prefer it that way if that's acceptable to you.

Why do you say things like that, God? "If that's acceptable to you"? What's that supposed to mean?? You're supposed to be God, you're supposed to make all the rules. You're supposed to tell us what to do, not ask if a thing is acceptable to us!

Yes, you're right, I do make the rules. And one of the most important rules I've made is that you make your own rules. You get to decide what sort of relationship we will have, because if you don't get to decide, it's not a relationship. If you'd understood that about our relationship when you came to this land, you wouldn't have tried to take control.

If you'd ignored Religion and listened to me, you would have understood. You would have understood that control does not build relationship. You get a choice, Mark – you can control someone, or you can have a relationship with them – but you can't have both.

For hundreds of years, you whites have sought to control every people you have engaged. And make no mistake, Māori have done exactly the same. It's what humans do when influenced by the dark forces, you seek to take control. But I brought you together as an opportunity for you both to learn a better way.

I do not try to colonise your heart. But the problem is that Religion has taught you exactly the opposite. Religion has taught you that I want control, that I want to colonise and take your life from you. What?? Haven't you read the scripture – it says that I *gave* my Son to the world, I didn't rip the world from you and give it to my Son. It says that I stand and knock waiting for you to invite me in. I don't kick down doors.

You sought to make your colonisation look nice so that it appeased your own religious double standards – a God who gave his life, but who also wants to take control – those are the double standards that Religion lies to you about. And so you attempt to do the same. You did it when you came here and you do it in your human relationships too. You come appearing gentle, but once established in a relationship you attempt to take control. That is not what I do.

But God, the Māori did that too – and waaay before we came.

Of course they did. All humans do. This is not a discussion about Pākehā being the bad guys and Māori the good. You're both the good guys in my estimation, but you both need to own the responsibility for moving forward. I wanted you to share. You need to talk about how, going forward, retaining your own unique strengths and cultures, you are going to work together. This is not a 'Māori thing', it's a 'Māori and Pākehā thing'. You're both in this. This story, your story, is a big bit brown and a big bit white. Saying sorry is a means to an end Mark, not the end itself. And guess what, Māori understand that better than you Pākehā do.

God, the thing is though, that every Māori has at least a little bit of white in them, so how does that fit with all this? Just saying.

Aaah, and every single one of you Pākehā, the longer you spend walking on this land, the more Māori you have in you. It cuts both ways. You are in them, and they in you. But… even with a little bit of Māori in you, you're still Pākehā, Mark. Each of you knows in your heart which you are. You're Pākehā. You want to stand up and haka and you would if you knew how, but you're Pākehā, white, and that's how I made you. And for you that's good. But for them it's not.

There's work to be done. Work that needs to be done by both of you together. The point of any repentance is restoration, getting back together. The problem has always been that neither of you knew how to listen to me. Both of you could easily have known, the knowledge was plainly held, hidden in plain sight by both sides. I wasn't on either side when you arrived, and I'm not on either side now. But I need both sides to join forces and get busy, as brothers, in the clean-up. Do you get that? Because it's about time you do. Both of you.

OK, so what's the first step, God?

Learn to listen to me. Properly. Not a smidgen here, and a nudge there. That's not enough, not nearly good enough. That's trying to listen to me with earmuffs on. Drop your religion and enter into a conversation with me, so that you can hear exactly what I'm saying to you both, as you move forward. Together.

'In the bonds of love we meet.' Oh really??

It can't be done without a conversation with me

God, I've been sensing that you want to talk about this, about haka and didgeridoos, for weeks.

Yes. You've been putting it off. We always end up talking about other things. You avoid this subject because you sense it's very deep and that frightens you.

But God, I thought each time we started talking about this, it was you who ended up wanting to talk about other things?? You talked about wild and fierce brothers, about two people with blood on their hands, about the wounded land – about squashing what another person is like.

Yes, I wanted to talk about those things but I also wanted to get to this subject, it's the core. The sound of the land and its people is the core. But Mark, a conversation with me is just that, it's a conversation, you can take the subject off in another direction if you want – and you've been doing that.

Yes, but you're God. Aren't you supposed to be in control – aren't you supposed to keep our minds on you – you know the whole 'God's on the throne' thing that us Christians love to say?

Yes, you've got the throne bit right, but the rest of it wrong. Of course I'm on the throne, but I'm in a lot of other places too – and in my kingdom the throne is not a place to rule and dominate from – and you're not a machine to be stuck on only one subject. You're human, you're self-determining, and I love that. In my kingdom the throne is a place to serve and love from. It was from the throne that I sent my son to die. It was from the throne I came to die. It was from the throne I came and accompanied, comforted and strengthened the One Who Died. Always from the throne we come, always to serve we come.

OK God, so you want to talk about the sound of the land and its people – and you're saying it's very deep?

Very deep.

How do you mean?

I mean it's deeply spiritual. At a level you aren't comfortable with. That's because you're white.

God, do you have to talk like that? I have a lot of readers who are white and some of them find this sort of thing offensive. It drags up so many political issues, God. Issues that I find myself siding with them on, at least half the time anyway.

Of course you do, you're white! That's how I made you.

OK, but you're talking almost as though you're brown, God.

I am brown! That caught you by surprise didn't it? I am brown, Mark, and I'm white. I'm white and brown. Remember I created you in my image, brown, yellow, red, black and white. So it's not rocket science, Mark – if all colours are copies of me, then I'm all colours.

Really, God?

Yes really. I'm very pleased that you're white, and they are brown.

For you white is exactly the right colour, it looks better on you, but for them brown looks much better. I like brown on them and white on you. Do you understand that?

Yes, in principle – I think so anyway?

Yes, you've got the rough idea, Mark, but none of you really understands because each of you views it from your own perspective. You try to see their brownness through your white eyes and they try to see your whiteness through their brown eyes. It doesn't really work, does it?

That's hardly either of our fault, God!! Actually, it's your fault. You gave me a white perspective and him a brown one.

Yes. I'm glad you're seeing that. At last!

What's that supposed to mean, God?? Anyone who knows you exist recognises that you created every race differently.

Yes. But not really, Mark. Each of you, brown and white, pretends that you understand but you don't. You're too different, and you've wounded each other too much. You say that you understand you're different, but you don't. As you seek to understand each other's differences, you look for the things in them that are like you – which sees you avoid the things that are different. You don't understand the things about each other that are different, how could you, you can't even see them!!

Each of you, when trying to understand the other, looks for common ground – but I don't want you to look for common ground – I want you to find the uncommon ground. To find it and champion it!! I want you to champion the things about the other that are completely different from you.

But you don't know how to do that. And that's what I want to talk to you about, and always will want to talk about. Neither of you, neither brown nor white has the ability to understand the uncommon things in the other. You have absolutely no frame of reference. You don't know about them because they're the things in the other person that are not like you!

When I brought you both to this land, I did it to teach you to understand each other because the things that you can't understand about the other will help you understand things you don't know about yourselves.

But how can we do that, God?? You just said that we can't.

Yes, I did.

Then what?? I don't get it.

Yes you do. Actually you do get it. You can hear me suggesting it all the time in the background as we have these conversations.

Really?

Really.

OK... well I'm pretty sure I can hear you saying that you brought us both to this land knowing that when we met each other, it would force us to talk to you. We would recognise that the other was so different from us that we would need to ask you how to understand them and to proceed in this relationship?

Yes. Exactly! The moment you ask me about the other person – if you ask me in a real back and forward conversation, I will open your eyes to the unlearnable things about them. And you need that. The whole purpose of relationship, any relationship, is to make you aware that you cannot hope to understand the other without me.

Relationship is designed to drive you to a conversation with me. A conversation where you are desperately aware that you need answers. Big answers! Without a proper conversation with me you will only be able to understand the things about them that are like you.

Are you honestly saying that, God?

Yes, of course I'm saying that. Any psychiatrist or psychologist worth their salt understands this. You may not, but they do. It's obvious. Looking for common ground only gives you common ground. You never venture into the wonderful territory of the things that make the other completely different from you.

The differences in another person are at the same time intoxicating and yet frightening. The differences are the real attractions, the mystery. That's love. And that's what I wanted and still want between the two of you, between brown and white. I want love. You have made a lie out of your national anthem; 'in the bonds of love we meet'. How can you possibly love each other if you don't understand each other??

How on earth can we understand each other, God?

I will teach you the unteachable things about each other. If each of you learned those unlearnable things about the other from me, then you would be able to teach each other.

So you want us to teach each other?

Yes.

But what, God?

What do you mean 'but what', Mark?

I mean, I can sense there's a 'but'.

Yes, you can. It's interesting isn't it, as you learn to converse with me you can hear my voice in your mind, but you can also sense the unspoken things – just as you would in a conversation with another human. In this case the 'but' is that I want you to learn to let the brown teach you before you teach them.

Why?

Because they won't teach you if you don't invite them to. Whether you want to admit it or not – and forget about all their 'faults' that you find so hard to understand – the fact remains that you have crushed their spirit. And the few whose spirit remains intact no longer trust you to listen. They are not prepared to teach you anymore because you have made it clear you are not willing to listen.

I brought you both here to teach each other. To teach each other the things about yourselves that the other cannot hope to understand. But each of you will always be deaf to the other's teaching until you learn to listen to me first. You need me to explain to you what the other is really saying.

That's the nature and purpose of relationship, Mark. You need me to explain to you what the other is saying. And this is where I want to talk about the didgeridoo and the sound of the desert – about the haka and the sounds of dense bush, rushing rivers and crashing surf.

OK?

Mark, you remember what David Garratt said about the aborigine man playing the digeridoo in the mall in Perth?

Yes, the man in the mall said that the sound of the didgeridoo was the sound of the desert.

And you understood, suddenly you understood didn't you??

Yes. Miriam and I rode our Harley through 2850 kms of Aussie desert

gravel, and all the time I could hear in my spirit the sound of the didgeridoo. The intense heat, the dust and flies, the stillness - yet somehow I could hear the didgeridoo.

But??

But I didn't understand what I was hearing. I didn't know how to put it into words until years later when David talked about what the Aborigine man had said to him about the sound of the desert.

Exactly!! You could hear it already, but suddenly you understood what you could hear. His simple instrument, the didgeridoo, taught you the beginning of what the Spirit is saying in the desert.

What spirit?

My Spirit, the Holy Spirit, me. You needed a person of the land to explain what you could hear me saying.

Really? Really that was you I could hear out in the desert on the Harley?

Of course. It was clearly spiritual, and the Spirit was me.

And the same goes for Māori, God? Is that what you're saying?

Yes. All peoples of the land are the same, they understand the sound of the land for the simple reason that they've been listening longer. Paul made that abundantly clear in Romans. But you never allowed them to teach you the deep spiritual meanings and sounds of this land.

And now, because you wouldn't listen to them, most of them have forgotten the meanings of the sounds.

What should we do?

Remind them and then listen to them!! Remind them that they once knew what I was saying through the sounds of the land. Ask them to remember the sounds and to teach you. They heard those sounds centuries before you did.

The sound of the land is the sound of me. I speak through the land. I say different things in every land, because although I am the same, each land I speak through is different.

Just as Paul explained in Romans, the land makes it clear what I am saying. You were supposed to ask them what I was saying through the land when you first arrived here. And it's not too late for you to ask. That's the correct order. It's an upside down sort of order. The indigenous people speaking first.

Why is it upside down?

Because it's the opposite of what you have always believed. You have always believed you belong at the top, in command. That's what you called yourselves, the 'colonists'. The ones who come to take away another's land in order to use it and have it for themselves. It's your own description of yourselves, Mark. It's time you wore another. And the way to start is to let them teach you first. Let them teach you what I was and still am saying through the land. Then, and only then, can you have your turn.

Māori and Pākehā Neither Is Complete Without The Other

God, did you honestly just say that?

Yes.

Are you sure? I didn't just make that up?

Why would you make a thing like that up?

Well, I wouldn't of course. It's not a nice thing to say. God, people are going to find that idea, to quote what it says in the Bible, 'a hard saying'.

They will. Many, to quote the Bible again, will 'stumble over it.'

Then why say it, for goodness sakes, God!?!

Truth divides, Mark.

What?? I thought you said truth unites.

It does.

Now I'm confused.

First truth divides. Like a surgeon, it divides in order to put the pieces back together properly. The enemy divides to conquer, whereas Truth divides in order to serve.

You said Truth divides in order to unite! Which is it, unite or serve?

Both, Mark. Hear me out. Your enemy wants to conquer Māori, and to conquer Pākehā, and he uses each of you to help him conquer the other. That's his nature. Cowardly. But I have come to serve you both – to serve Māori and to serve Pākehā. That's my nature. I am the God who serves.

I want to use each of you to help me serve the other. Pākehā serving Māori, Māori serving Pākehā, and me on each of the serving teams. That will take huge courage for both Māori and Pākehā, far more courage than it takes to fight each other. I want you to fight but on the same side against the invisible enemy who tricks you to fight each other. As you serve each other and learn to fight on the same side against your mutual enemies, Truth will unite you. You need each other, Mark. You need the other to complete you. Pākehā were called here by me because I knew that those I called here would be completed by Māori. And I called Māori here to prepare the way for you, to be here ready for you to complete them.

Hang on, God, we moved away from a key thing you said there. You said that many people would find this a hard concept and that they would stumble over it.

Of course, it is a hard saying. There are many wounds. On both sides. Both sides believe the other has wounded them more grievously. Both sides are astounded that the other could think that they are the aggrieved party. And that is the nature of relationship when the enemy gets involved. And the enemy always gets involved in relationship, Mark. Always. The enemy persuades you that the other is more at fault. You saw it from the first two key relationships – Adam blamed Eve and Cain blamed Abel. They were taught that response by the filth, Mark. The vile one is always working to destroy relationship and he has done a fine job in the case of Māori and Pākehā. Both of you pretending respect for the other, both of you unsure, at best, in the other's company. It has to stop.

That sounds a bit stern?

Not at all. I am not the demanding God. I am the God who serves. I'm simply saying that for both of your sakes, and if you want to move on together, it has to stop.

So what do we need to do?

Listen to each other. You listen first. Let Māori speak. Encourage them to speak. Insist that they speak without commanding them to do so. No one gets to command. I am the Commander of the armies of the Lord of Hosts, the Commander who comes serving, but nevertheless the Commander.

But Mark, let's also speak of those who will find these things to be hard sayings and stumble over them. You can do nothing about that. I can do very little either. People in high places, a number of Christians in authority, will find these things too challenging to accept. You can do nothing about that, but you can serve those who can hear my voice and want to respond to what I am doing. It's getting late, Mark, time is marching on, this was supposed to happen from 200 years ago onwards. It's time you got started.

God, I'm hearing the words to that Bob Dylan song. But that will just make those people in high places even crosser. They're going to think it's deception that you might speak about such important subjects through a secular song.

I speak through whatever you are listening to, Mark, and that's part of what you listen to. 'the times they are changing...'

Well, I can't quite remember it God, but there's that line in that song that says something about 'if you can't lend a hand get out of the way'.

Yes, Mark. People need to know I'm saying this. I have work to do with Māori and Pākehā. Your relationship needs an overhaul, but most of the overhauling we can do as we set out and get busy together. The time for 'sorry' is all but over. There will need to be more sorries as we go forward, but the time now is to plan for war. Two fierce tribes, brown and white, fighting invisible armies together. And you haven't got a hope if you don't know how to converse with me and hear me give you step by step, blow by blow instructions on the names of your enemies and how best to fight them.

And that's what I'm saying to anyone who knows how to listen. I'm doing something with your two peoples just like Bob wrote. Please heed the call. Don't (whatever you do) stand in the doorway, don't block up the hall because the ones who get hurt will be those who stall.

I won't hurt you, but you will be left behind by the changes that I am making. My advice? Embrace the things I called both of you to this land to do. I called you to listen to each other, to serve each other and then, with true courage and the wild hearts of brown and white, mount up and follow me. To the battle, your enemy approaches and he wastes no time!!

Want To Know How To Have Your Own Conversations With God About This Subject?

See back section of this book: Page 181

"What they never told you about how to have a back and forth conversation with God"

Māori And Pākehā Have An Opportunity That Every Generation Has Had

Every generation of Māori and Pākehā,
for 200 plus years, has had this same opportunity
– and yet none has ever seized it

God, today I'm driving along, minding my own business, and I think you said...

I did say.

OK, well, you did say... Are you sure, God? Are you sure you said that?

Totally sure.

OK, that's pretty definite then I guess...

Very definite, Mark.

OK, what I heard you say was simply this – actually now that I try to say it out loud, it's not that simple after all.

Give it a go, Mark.

OK, well, I think I heard you say...

I did say, Mark.

OK, I did hear you say that us Pākehā and Māori in this generation, those of us alive right now, we have an opportunity that no other

generation has ever had.

Not quite. You're nearly right, but not quite. What you actually heard me say was this: You Pākehā and Māori, those of you alive right now, you have an opportunity that every other generation of Māori and Pākehā has had since you Pākehā first arrived. And yet no generation until now, has ever seized this opportunity, none has ever taken advantage of it. None. And here it is again, Mark, the opportunity is here once again. The opportunity to start this journey together, the Māori and Pākehā journey. The opportunity to start it is right here, right now.

This is the journey I wanted the two of you to start, a partnership, a way to show the world how to dance the delicate dance of melding two cultures, of mixing two peoples. Not one dominating the other, but the two operating in partnership. That journey. That journey is here right now, the train is at the station and the doors are open – the waka (canoe) is anchored in the shallows and there are whawhai waka ama (paddle) for all who will grab and use one.

The opportunity is here at last, here at last once again. Just as it has been presented, here at last, to every new generation since you first arrived. Here it is yet again. Will you take it? Will you start this journey?

It's time, Mark. If you shun it, if Māori and Pākehā alike say this is too hard, then it will wait for your children, and for theirs, but here's your chance, Mark. Here's the chance for this generation to count and stand out from all the others. Here's the chance for your generation, Māori and Pākehā, to say let's get on this train, let's get in this waka together and get started. Your chance to be the generation that men will stand up and call blessed. The generation that taught the world what I wanted to teach the world when you Pākehā first arrived. 200 plus years ago. First I called Māori here eons before you, and then you too, to join them. Two peoples. Aaah two peoples.

(At this point they stop talking to me, The Three stop talking to me and I can hear them talking to each other, The Three Mighty Ones, the Eternal ones, I can hear them sighing and musing about the beauty of the picture of the melding of our two peoples. It's such a powerful moment that even I am a bit scared to talk. But I do... :( )

Umm, should I just wait while you talk?

No no, this needs to be said. The moment is now. It has been now a number of times down through the years, and now here it is again. The moment is now again. Aaah. It is here again and we can hear the land crying for it. Can you hear that, Mark? Listen. The land is singing to you both that the moment is now, once again it is now. Listen, Mark. The land is singing this moment. You can feel and hear the power of the land. Listen to the land, it sings my purposes.

Luke 19: 40 (Jesus talking to the disciples) He replied, "If they kept quiet, the stones along the road would burst into cheers!"

The moment to do what, God? What moment is the land singing into being for us – it is isn't it? That's what you're saying? The land is singing this new and powerful moment into being for us??

Yes. *(Isaiah 55:12 Ka pakaru mai te waiata a ngā maunga, a ngā pukekuke, i tō koutou aroaro – the mountains and the hills will burst into song before you.)*

Yes. The moment is here now. Here it comes! The moment to move ahead together. The moment to be mighty together. Aaah. The moment to be mighty together. The moment to rise up and conquer the joint woes of your two people. Them showing you the way, then you showing them the way. The moment to learn from each other. To move forward. To listen to each other. Listen to them first. They have given up talking to you because you won't listen. That's all. It's just that they're afraid to speak to you because it would be words wasted. Listen, Mark. LISTEN. L i s t e n. Encourage them to speak, and then listen.

You're back on that sunny beach again, Mark. On so many beaches; Marsden's Christmas at Oihi, Tasman's 'Murderer's Bay' at Whariwharangi. The meeting of many at Waitangi. So many meetings – you're back there at all of them. Māori and Pākehā, you're back there again – will you seize the day? This is your chance, this generation's chance to have those meetings again. To talk. To make a difference. To rewrite history!! To teach each other. To listen. To feel and learn the power of the other and to combine forces. To fight the invisible enemy. To show the world how to mix two great peoples.

The two great peoples that I called together, and am still calling. Together. Two proud and wonderful peoples. Aaah. The power, the combined might of the two of you. Hear it calling down from ages past. Hear the land sing, Mark. Hear it sing.

Want To Know How To Have Your Own Conversations With God About This Subject?

See back section of this book: Page 181

"What they never told you about how to have a back and forth conversation with God"

The Very Land You Walk On Is Alive

God, I'm pretty sure you told me a few days ago that the land is alive.

Yes.

Oh man, God!!! I'm really hoping I heard that wrong.

Why? What's the problem?

It sounds so weird, God.

Yes it does, Mark. To you it sounds weird. European cultures don't easily understand this. You Europeans are far too logical a people to relate easily to an idea like the land being alive.

Does that mean it's not a logical idea?

Mark, it's very logical. All truth is logical.

But?

But you cannot see it, so it seems illogical to you. That's how you Europeans are.

Is that bad?

Not at all, that's how I made you. No one people group has the whole truth. I would never allow that, you would become too powerful. The need to gain more truth and greater knowledge keeps each people group focused and less dangerous to themselves and others.

> **GEN 11:1-7** *"the LORD came down to see the city and the tower which the sons of men had built. And the LORD said, "Indeed the people are one and they all have one language, and this is what they begin to do; now nothing that they propose to do will be withheld from them. Come, let Us go down and there confuse their language, that they may not understand one another's speech." So the LORD scattered them abroad from there over the face of all the earth."*

You Europeans are hungry for logic and strategy. Whereas indigenous peoples are more intuitive, more able to see and understand things that cannot be seen. That balances them, every race is given strengths that balance them to keep them from becoming too powerful. Indigenous peoples are often more courageous, more likely to fight to the death – imagine if they were also as fond of logic as you. It would make them too powerful. Every people group must have an equal chance.

As I said, Pākehā and Māori need each other and that, not the theft of land or the subjugation of culture, is why I brought you together, but that's not the purpose of this conversation. More of that another time.

OK, I'm getting lost. What's this conversation supposed to be about?

It can be about whatever you want it to be about. I am happy to talk about any subject you want to discuss.

No!! God, how many times do I have to tell you that I want to know what you want to talk about??

Alright, fine. If you insist, we'll talk about what I want to talk about. The land, Mark. The land is alive.

> **Isa. 55:12** *"The mountains and hills will burst into song before you, and all the trees of the field will clap their hands."*
>
> **Gen. 4:10** *The Lord said, "What have you done? Listen! Your brother's blood cries out to me from the ground. Now you are cursed from the ground which has opened her mouth to receive your brother's blood from your hand. From now on the ground will not yield its strength to you."*
>
> **Luke 19:40** *"I tell you," he replied, "if they keep quiet, the stones will cry out."*
>
> **Rom. 8:22** *"For we know that the whole creation has been moaning together as in the pains of childbirth until now."*
>
> **Ps. 19:1** *"The heavens declare ['Saphar': Recount. Relate. Tell] the glory of God; the skies proclaim the work of his hands."*

Yes. That's what I thought you said a few days ago. But it's a difficult concept, God. It sounds like mumbo jumbo. And I can tell you right now that a number of my Pākehā/European readers are going to be unhappy and uncomfortable with this idea. But you're saying that's because they and I are white and we don't relate easily to an idea like that?

That's what I'm saying. The land is alive, Mark. That offends your European sensibilities because you can't easily see it – I have created you that way – if you can't see something, you find it difficult to understand. And like any attribute I build into a people, that's a good thing. That particular characteristic drives you Europeans to find out how a thing works. Modern science is founded on those strengths, your great need to see what's really going on. You refuse to accept the way things are, instead you want to know how a thing works and why.

And so?

And so your scientists are already discovering that the land is alive. Things they are uncovering are pointing to the incontrovertible truth that the land is alive, a living thing. It won't be long before it's an accepted concept and widely known by the common man in western European society.

Then can't we wait till they prove it, why do you have to tell me now? You're just making me look like a kook, God!

Because you need to understand it now while it's still not widely accepted or known.

Why?

Because of the things that are to come and that have been.

God, that sounds very weird and mystical – like a line out of Lord of the Rings.

Yes, it does doesn't it?

You didn't say that, God!!

Yes, I did. I agree it does sound weird and mystical. And there's a reason for that.

Where on earth is this conversation going, God?

All over the place. Are you comfortable with that?

What choice do I have, God??

Every choice. If you want to talk about something else, you go right ahead. I came to serve and I always fit in with whatever you want the subject to be. You see that constantly in organised Christianity.

You come together, you name the topic, I turn up and fit in.

Wow. OK, I choose to continue with this topic.

Good. What we're talking about sounds mystical, like something out of Lord of the Rings, because as told in that story, much of the wisdom that you humans need is already in the land, on it and above it – it's in the elements, in 'nature'.

Ps. 19:1-3 *"Heaven makes heard the glory of God and the firmament shows the work of his hands. Day unto day pours forth speech; night unto night shows knowledge. There is no speech nor words whose voice will not be heard."*

Life is so much simpler than your white European culture wants it to be.

Here we go again, God, we're back to the whole indigenous thing again, aren't we.

To an extent, yes. Is that alright with you?

I guess. It's just that I'm so out of my depth with it.

What better reason to teach you about it.

You know what, God? You're impossible. I mean, when you say things like that you're lovable, but at the same time completely impossible.

Like a woman, were you thinking Mark?

Yes, like a woman. That's what I was thinking, God.

Yes.

What's that supposed to mean?

That's a whole conversation in itself, Mark. The similarities between me and a woman. You want me to be male, but given that women too are created in my image then it stands to reason, even for you logical Pākehā, that much of my personality is female. Sorry, but that's the truth.

Can we just talk about the subject that we started out talking about please God?

That's a very white male sort of attitude, Mark.

Well, that's what I am, God. You made me that way.

Yes, I did. And I'm happy with that choice. But that doesn't mean you're complete like you are. You need the knowledge that comes from women, and from indigenous people – from them, from the land and from me. The knowledge that isn't already in you. Do you understand that?

Not really.

No. But you're beginning to. Stick with it, Mark.

OK, well God, I'm fairly sure that I will have lost half my white male readers by now! We're supposed to be talking about the land and the fact that it's alive. That subject alone will put them off. A normal rational white male doesn't like to think about that sort of thing.

No, you don't. Your love of logic at the cost of wisdom is one of the subtopics of this conversation, but let's stick with the main topic. The land is alive.

As I said, people aren't going to like that idea, God.

No. A lot of them won't. Indigenous people already know the land is alive, Mark, the old ones do, and the younger ones find it easy enough to pick up on. But you're right, you Pākehā find it a difficult concept and you white Christians have the worst time of all trying to relate to it.

Why?

Because you believe that if you don't already know about a thing, if it's not already a common teaching, then it must be wrong.

Why?

Because you think that if the Bible doesn't talk about a thing it cannot be true.

Isn't that true?

The Bible talks about almost every subject, but like any manual, it can be easily misinterpreted. A group of Christians reject a particular truth because 'it's not in the Bible' they say, and then a generation or two later that same group embraces that truth because they realise that actually yes, it is in the Bible after all. People shape what the Bible says to fit what they already believe. That's the nature of humanity.

Do we have to become more expert at the Bible?

Yes. But expertise alone counts for nothing. The Pharisees were the most expert of any generation at knowing the scriptures, but they were also the generation that most completely misunderstood what the scriptures were saying.

> **John 5:39** *"You study the Scriptures diligently because you think that in them you have eternal life. These are the very Scriptures that testify about me, yet you refuse to come to me to have life."*

I want you to learn more and more scripture but I want you to learn it direct from me.

What do you mean?

I mean ask me what it means. Allow me to interpret it for you. Only learn it as fast as you can hear me interpret it. Learning it without me – it is only words.

> **2 COR 3:6** *"for the letter ['Gramma' A written document, an epistle, writings] kills, but the Spirit gives life."*

Want To Have Your Own Back And Forth Conversation With God About Māori, Pākehā And The Land?

See back section of this book: Page 181

Includes: Six amazing interviews with God about how to have your own conversation with him. Hear what God has to say to you about all this.

People In Authority Who Shift Boundaries Without Permission, Curse The Land And The People

God, yesterday morning – we were away for the weekend – I went out early for a walk and something unusual happened. I wasn't ready for it at all. As soon as my feet touched the ground I heard the word 'Poverty'. It was as though the word came up out of the ground.

Yes.

And yet when I asked you if it was you who had said the word poverty, I think you said no?

You're right. I did say no, it wasn't me who said poverty.

But then later, the people we were staying with told us that the area is in dire poverty. That the New Zealand Government recognises the area is endangered and that poverty is rife.

Yes.

Well, I don't get it, God. First I hear the word 'Poverty'. Then when I ask if you said it, you say no. And then the local people tell us the area is drowning in poverty and you tell me they're right.

Yes, they are right. More right than even they realise.

So why did you tell me that it wasn't you who said 'Poverty' to me.

Because it wasn't me. I didn't say poverty, your enemy did. Yes, that area is in poverty, yes, the land cries out poverty, but no, it's not me saying it. Your enemy has cursed the area and spoken the word poverty over it. And now the very land itself cries out poverty. The land cries out at the wound of the curse put on it by the enemy. The land cries out poverty, and the enemy shouts poverty back at the land.

I think I can hear you saying to ask how or why the enemy put the curse on the land?

Yes.

How did the enemy put the curse of poverty on the land?

Greedy people used their power and authority to shift boundaries without the permission of those who owned the land.

I don't understand.

Two things happen when you shift boundaries, Mark. The first is that one property gets smaller and so has less area to support the same enterprise and people. The second effect is a far deeper principle. It is the real issue. I created the land in a way that it would adapt and rearrange itself to work with the people who live on it. The land is alive, Mark. Yes, I know that offends your intelligence, but make no mistake, it's true.

And being alive it responds to the people who live on it. It adapts to the boundaries set by the people living on it. I've designed it that way, a wonderful relationship between the land which is alive and the people who live on it.

The land develops a life and a 'heart' that beats within the boundaries set, and responds to those living within those boundaries. A piece of land has a heart and a life, and then when people agree to halve that land so that one piece becomes two, the land adapts again, rearranges itself. A piece of land that once had one heart, develops two hearts because now it is two pieces of land. That's a good thing. I have designed the land to be that way. The land actually recognises and responds to boundaries established in honesty. Once again, that offends your intelligence, but once again, it is also true.

Land welcomes more people to live on it and is happy to be divided and reorganised, and it adapts to suit these new arrangements. The people and their land work together. It's a mystery, but that's enough of an explanation for now.

So it's OK to change boundaries?

Yes, absolutely. I have created the land to welcome more and more people. I want the population to grow. And people need land, a place. The land, beautiful when it is empty, is also beautiful when it is filled with people – but only if the dividing up and allocation of the land is done honestly and with honour. Greed upsets the balance. The land, which groans to see the humans on it listen to me, is hurt when they don't. The single purpose of the land on which you live is a place for you to have a conversation with me – a gift from me to make conversation easier.

Rom 8:22 *'For the creation waits in eager expectation for the children of God to be revealed.'*

Rom 8:19 *'For those who are led by the Spirit of God are the children of God.'*

When you shift boundaries dishonestly or by force, you wound those who live on that land and you wound their land too. Wounded and cursed, the land cannot rearrange itself properly, its heart or other 'organs' cannot develop properly or are wounded and do not function properly. The land is 'sick'. When you appropriate a people's land by shifting boundaries dishonestly or without permission, you steal from them.

John 10:10 *'The robber comes only to steal, kill and destroy.*

You join hands with Satan, and although you may only have intended to extend your own borders, you have become the robber – the robber who comes 'to steal, kill and destroy.' Small, seemingly justified and almost innocent moments of historical greed have huge implications on future generations. When you steal land you destroy people. You take away their soul. They and their land are both destroyed.

And Mark, Satan loves that. He delights in it. The Church teaches that Satan is most focused on tempting you to naughty sins, but he is far more cunning than that. He seeks to destroy your very soul. He takes a little bit of greed and carefully manipulates a man to dishonestly extend his borders and laughs to himself as he sees the destruction to generations of people that this will bring.

And of course your enemy is safe in his plans because those who extend their borders are satisfied and not about to reveal the secret of their theft, in fact, over generations they come to justify and 'legalise' their theft in their own minds. They see the benefits to themselves and they rest and say "it is good". The generations who follow them onto the land that they have stolen have no reason to question the benefits they inherit.

Those whose land is stolen are wounded, confused and bewildered and do not fully recognise what has happened to them. They are left powerless and because they feel powerless their soul begins to seep out of them. One generation follows another on to the wounded land. The curse on the land curses those born on to it, and the curse on them curses the land afresh.

You're saying something about the church here aren't you?

Mark, the established church has blessed this and been deeply involved in it down through the ages. The church has always accompanied the organisations and governments that have moved to new places to acquire land – whether peacefully or in war. They have blessed those who have acquired land – both honestly and dishonestly – and they have refused to discern between the two.

The masons are only part of the devious, secretive, whitewashed destruction of people by taking their land. The church is implicated at every level, 'up to their eyeballs in it' as you would say. The church historically, has whitewashed the theft, blessed it, justified it, saying that this has benefitted those whose land has been stolen. It says they were not able to manage the land and that they and the land are better off having 'godly' church members owning and managing it. And of course, the church has benefitted financially too.

Is this peculiar to the established Christian church?

In the western world, yes. But the spirit behind the church, that great and powerful principality called Religion, has used many other organised religions to do the same. Judaism, the Incas, Asia – in every country the state or state-recognised religions have blessed and aided the rich and powerful in their drive to extend their borders. Religion and his many fawning and obedient organisations have whitewashed and 'made honest' the wholesale theft of land and the destruction of people through the sly shifting of borders, or confiscation by force, war and bloodshed.

And he and his invisible minions shriek with laughter at the double injustice of convincing those whose land has been stolen, to then embrace the church that blessed the theft. And so they become the prisoners both of its intent and of the organisation itself. It steals from them at every level. It takes their land, their soul, their weekly wages and their children.

The enemy pronounces curses over the land. He loves to do it because it destroys not only the land itself but the people on it.

And the enemy has spoken the word 'Poverty' over the area you visited yesterday, and now the land itself cries out poverty in pain and warning.

What are we supposed to do about that?

What do you think, Mark?

I don't know. I didn't think repentance was going to solve the problem and now I hear Māori say that it doesn't. And God, the theft of land and the shifting of boundaries is not just a Pākehā thing, it's been going on here and in every other nation for thousands of years.

Exactly.

So what should we do, God?

The first step is to recognise it. The first step is to recognise that for centuries, in this land and on every other land, there has been injustice after injustice – the shifting of boundaries, the cursing of the land and the people on it. No people is free from guilt. And running into church or taking cover under the memory of a wrong done against you, does not make your part in it go away, Mark. It's a mess.

The church has blessed it, aided it, repented for it, ignored it, pretended it is no longer an issue, but I'm not asking you Christians to decide what to do about it, I'm asking you to ask me. And there is no single 'one-size-fits-all' solution. Everyone, the wronged and the perpetrators, need to listen to me. You will not even know which you are – you will not know whether you are the perpetrator or the one who has been wronged – often you are both – unless you listen to me.

Its Time To Go Back To The Beaches And Talk

And talk and talk and talk
Ko te wā ka haere hoki ki te onē, ma te korero

OK, so God, am I right that you've had something you want to say all day?

Mark, I've always got something I've wanted to say all day.

What's that supposed to mean?

Exactly what it says, Mark. I've got plenty to say, plenty I've been wanting to say for at least a day, often a thousand days, often a thousand years.

OK. This is getting a little big. I'm not sure if I'm ready to hear stuff you've been wanting to say for a thousand years, God? Man alive, you get so serious so quickly!!!

Alright, Mark, let's start with what I've been wanting to say to you all day today.

OK?

It's time to go back to the beaches and talk. And talk. And talk. And talk and talk and talk.

Who?

You and them.

Who's you?

You Pākehā.

Oh man God, really? This again.

This again.

And I'm guessing 'them' is them Māori?

Them Māori. The very same. It's time you and them, Pākehā and Māori, went back to the beaches and talked. High time. It's getting late.

You want to explain this a little more, right?

You're *very* right. Listen, Mark.

OK?

When you first came, you Pākehā, you had to get out of your ships, hop into a boat, row to shore, and then get out of the boat and walk up the beach.

God, we've already talked about this, you and me.

Yes, we have. Was anyone listening?

I don't know. Were they?

Yes, some. For some my talk about the beaches was like a lightning bolt, others didn't quite understand. It needs to be said again. And again. And again and again. And then again.

Oh dear.

Yes, oh dear. So here we are saying it again. I want you to go back to the beaches.

Us Pākehā?

Yes and them. And Māori too. Back then you were both on the beaches. You arriving, them warding their land and cautiously welcoming you, testing to see if you came in peace, testing to see what you had in mind, and they were wrong. Many of them were wrong.

What do you mean?

Many of them thought you came in peace. They believed you.

We did didn't we?

You came to colonise, Mark. You came to acquire their land through fair means or foul. You came to take over. You thought they deserved that. You thought they would be better for it. You thought they understood that you and your God were superior. You thought they knew it and were welcoming you at that level. But they weren't.

They thought you came in peace. Many of them did. But they were wrong. Right from the start you intended that they would serve you. Not all of you thought that, but most did. You had been taught to think that was the right way. You knew no better. But they did. They would have taught you, had you listened. You thought that 'brown would serve white' was the model. Let me ask you though, Mark. Do you honestly think that was my intention? Could that possibly honestly have been my intention?

I guess not.

Of course not. And do you think that they, this proud people, these fierce brothers of yours, do you honestly think that they would have accepted that they should serve you without resistance?

Umm no?

Of course no. You can see them, you have seen their fierce nature, can you imagine what they were like back then, untainted by white custom – a fierce and proud people. Do you honestly think they would accept that their place was to serve you without a fight?

I guess not.

Aaaah. Trick question, Mark. Actually, this fierce, wild and dangerous people would have been prepared to serve you, more than ready to serve you provided one thing had been true. What do you think it was, that secret? The thing that would have prompted them to willingly serve you?

I'm lost here, God.

No you're not, you can hear it in your spirit, speak it out, Mark. Speak out the words. The land, the very land beneath your feet needs to hear this spoken by human voice. Many human voices.

OK. I think I can hear you saying that if we'd been prepared to serve them, they would have been prepared to serve us.

Say it again, Mark. Say it again.

Alright then... if we'd served them, they'd have served us.

Exactly. How hard was that to figure out?

Well, to be honest it was pretty hard, it must have been because we never did it.

Of course not. You didn't know how to listen to me, so how would you know? How could you possibly know what to do back on that beach when you didn't know then, and still don't know how, to listen to me. But I'm saying it now, Mark... You need to go back to the beaches, Mark, and talk. You and them.

Imagine this, Mark; imagine you're there back on the beaches, lots of beaches. Pākehā landing and walking cautiously up the beach. Māori waiting at the top of the beach. Cautiously. Wondering. You wondering about them, them wondering about you. Each of you intrigued and not a little fearful about the other. It sounds like the beginning of a marriage, Mark. Or a war. Which is it going to be? You've tried the war. First an aggressive bloody war, and then a cold and quiet war for a century and a half. It's time to start again. Is it going to be a marriage this time or another war?

So here you are again. There you are on the beaches. You coming up the beach, them standing at the top. Each recognising that the other is dangerous, as equally dangerous as you. Two dangerous people embarking on a relationship. Each wondering how this is going to go. Each recognising the other has the power to destroy you. And they do. And you do.

That's where I have you now, Mark. Both of you. And that's where I had you back then. They saw your magnificent weaponry and dogged persistence. A scrawny white people, underfed because that's how many of you were when you arrived. Unprepared and yet willing to come ashore and try your hand. And you seeing them, recognising that they were powerful and above you (the top of the beach is always above the shore). You walking up the beach to them realising they could take you. Them seeing you coming up the beach and recognising that with your ability to build such ships, you just might be able to take them. Two equal people. Equally dangerous.

Aaah. What a wonderful start to a relationship. Power to serve, rather than dominate. You came to take their land, but Mark, here's the rub. Here's what it says... The meek shall inherit the earth.

You were supposed to talk. Supposed to cautiously proceed and build a unique and powerful relationship. A relationship that was, and still is, meant to stand as testament on how to meld two cultures. Two people who needed each other. Neither thought that the case, but each of you could have taught the other the truth of the matter.

I called them here. And then I called you here. Neither of you is complete without the other. And yet here you are 200 plus years later and still… still you have not begun to talk.

That's what I have been waiting to say, Mark. Is anyone listening?? Only time will tell. And time, if you do not begin to talk, will win. It's time, Mark. Time will not wait. If you don't do it then the time, which is now, will have passed.

Korero. Talk. And talk. Me te korero. Ake ake ake.

Talk, talk and talk. For as long as it takes, and it will take forever.

Want To Know How To Have Your Own Conversations With God About This Subject?

See back section of this book: Page 181

"What they never told you about how to have a back and forth conversation with God"

God, what do you think about The Treaty of Waitangi?

I think a lot about it.

Why?

Because I always think a lot about agreements between people. When you have forgotten your agreements, I haven't. I never forget any agreement. I trust you. When two people make an agreement, I trust them to honour it. I'm there. I'm listening. The concept of agreement is a concept that I like. I invented it. An agreement is a bond between people to honour each other in some way, and it's made by choice. I like it when people have a choice.

I don't like it when they don't. I don't like domination, subjugation, force or condemnation. I don't practise any of those things. So for that reason, I'm always listening for and watching for agreements – arrangements and relationships where freedom of choice is the foundation.

That was a big answer for a little question, God – all I wanted to know is what you think about the Treaty of Waitangi.

That's what I think, Mark. And your question was not a 'little' question at all. Agreements are one of the foundations of life. They are the basis of our relationship in the Trinity, the three of us – our relationship is based on agreement. So we love it when you make agreements too.

Mark, the Treaty of Waitangi was an agreement that both parties wanted. For different reasons. The Māori wanted sovereignty over their own lands and the right to govern themselves. The right to keep their land or sell it. When they decided, not when you did. That's no surprise, that's what all humans want. The surprise to them was that you granted what they wanted.

What do you mean by that, God? Why were they surprised?

Simple, Mark. You have to remember who the Māori were, Mark. A nation of warriors. A nation of many kings who regularly went to war against each other. They understood better than you the rules of war and the conqueror and the conquered. They had lived by those rules for centuries. The most powerful force makes the rules, they understood that.

They were already beginning to suspect that if you kept coming in the numbers you seemed capable of, that they would soon be outnumbered and outmanned. They knew that they were stronger and more muscular, faster than you, but they also knew that you had better strategy, weaponry and scale. Your technology was far beyond theirs and they could see that. So they were amazed when you agreed to Treaty with them and guarantee them the possession and sovereignty over their own lands. They were amazed but they trusted you and took you at your word.

Now you tell me, Mark, what do I think of the Treaty of Waitangi?

That's a very dangerous question, God, I'd rather you answered it.

First, let me ask you another question; the Māori, although amazed at your willingness to allow them possession and sovereignty, nonetheless they trusted you...

How can I possibly know if that's true, God? I wasn't there!! They certainly don't seem to trust us now, so maybe I'm not hearing this correctly. Maybe they didn't trust us.

That wasn't my question, Mark, you can take my word on that; for the most part they trusted you. They could see there was something about you, something that made you equal to them, smaller, weaker, whiter, but your strategy, technology and dogged determination showed them they had met their match. I showed them that, I wanted them to see it, I wanted a partnership of two equal brothers – brown and white. You intrigued them, and then you offered to protect and allow them their rights, and so they trusted you.

OK, so what's your question, God?

Do you think you honoured your promise to them?

Oh God, don't start this! Possibly not, maybe not?? How would I know, God? Well, probably not always anyway, but it's past, God, it's a new day.

Oh, really Mark? When did this 'new day' dawn? Who decided it had dawned? When did the day of the promises you had made to each other finish and this 'new day' begin? And, Mark, who decided on what terms you should move on, who decided what the new rules should be? And are those new rules the rules of broken promises, or new promises?

God, if this is you, then why haven't you told us white Christians this before now?

Tell me a little bit about my nature, Mark? You know what I'm talking about.

OK, well, you don't push your will on us. You wait.

Yes. What do I wait for?

Well, God, this sounds ridiculous, but you wait for our permission.

Yes.

So, God, what you're saying is that you haven't talked about the Treaty of Waitangi to us white Pākehā Christians because we haven't given you permission?

No, you haven't. You haven't even asked me about it. Why would you? Until recently, your Government has been very happy with their actions surrounding the Treaty. Whatever the Government is happy with, you Christians have always been happy with too. You have enjoyed centuries of English history where Government and Christianity have been happy bedfellows. If your government has been for a people, then you Christians have been for them too – if they have been against a people, then you Christians have been against them too.

And what do you think, Mark? Has your government been for or against Māori for the most part of your history?

Do you really want me to answer that, God?

Yes, but not yet. I just want you to think about it. I want you to think about the actions of your government surrounding the treaty.

But, God, in recent years the Government has tried to honour the Treaty.

Yes, exactly. In recent years. And that has been good, but as I said, Mark, you white Christians didn't really start thinking much about it until, once again, your Government led the way. And if they hadn't led the way, you wouldn't have thought about it. You white Christians get your direction from the government. Your predominantly white church certainly does too.

White Christians and the church have not really asked me what I think about the Treaty. Why would you? You're comfortable with things the way they are.

This is sounding very one sided, God. You're sounding very Māori.

I am, Mark. I am Māori. I am Māori to the core. And I'm white. Whiter than you. I am all peoples. You have all come from me.

> **Eph. 3:14-15** *'the Father, from whom every family in heaven and on earth derives its name.'*

OK, wow. I don't know where to go, God.

Why not listen to me? Why not ask me??

OK ,what do you want to say about all this?

What verse can you hear in your heart, Mark? You've heard this verse a lot lately as you've heard me talk about Māori and Pākehā. This has a lot to do with what I think about the Treaty of Waitangi.

Oh man, God! Do we have to talk about that?

Not at all. You don't have to do anything you don't want to.

Oh, lets not start with that, God!! OK, the verse I'm hearing, the verse I keep hearing whenever I think about the relationship between us Whites and Māori, is from where you were speaking to Cain after he killed Abel.

Yes. That's me reminding you of that verse, Mark. Read it out.

> **Gen 4:9-10** *"Then the Lord said to Cain, "Where is your brother Abel?" "I don't know," he replied. "Am I my brother's keeper?" The Lord said, "What have you done? Listen! Your brother's blood cries out to me from the ground."*

So God, when I hear that verse, I feel a deep sadness somehow. So I'm guessing you're saying us whites were in the wrong. That we dishonoured the Treaty and murdered Māori and that somehow they were our brothers.

They are your brothers, Mark.

So is that what you're saying? That us Pākehā were in the wrong?

Not so fast, Mark. We're not talking about right or wrong just yet. That's where you Christians, (Pākehā or Māori) think I always want to go. You think I'm always focused on right and wrong.

Well, aren't you?

No. I'm focused on people.

OK, well if you don't want to talk about right or wrong, what do you want to talk about?

I want to talk about people. About Māori and Pākehā and the Treaty of Waitangi.

Why?

Because you asked about it.

So let's say I want you to keep talking about it, what else do you want to say about it?

I want you to tell me what you think about it, Mark. What do you think about the Treaty of Waitangi?

I think I don't know enough about it. I think that sometimes I think that we were very unfair. I think I'm shocked when I discover there were two versions, an English version and a Māori version, and the Māori version had us guaranteeing them the right to keep all their land, to be in control of the sale of the land, to not have to sell it unless

they wanted to. The Māori version guaranteed them sovereignty over their lands, their villages and their treasures. I think it guaranteed them sovereignty and self rule to some extent. And we wrote the Māori version, they didn't. It sounds like we were a bit shifty, God? We gave them one version, but actually we ourselves acted more on the other version. That's what I think anyway. But I'm not sure I want to think those things. After all, I'm white God. It's uncomfortable to think those things.

Yes. Close enough, Mark. You've got a little bit of that wrong, but the spirit of what you're saying is true. So you tell me, have you honoured that?

Umm, God, I've looked up the Ministry of Justice's view on the Treaty of Waitangi and it says this;

"Article 2 of the Treaty of Waitangi
"The Māori version of article 2 uses the word 'rangatiratanga' in promising to uphold the authority that tribes had always had over their lands and taonga. This choice of wording emphasises status and authority."

"As a result, in this article, Māori believed they ceded to the Queen a right of governance in return for the promise of protection, while retaining the authority they always had to manage their own affairs."

"In the English text, the Queen guaranteed to Māori the undisturbed possession of their properties, including their lands, forests, and fisheries, for as long as they wished to retain them."

This text emphasises property and ownership rights, God, this is dangerous ground. I better not be hearing this wrong. I better not let any perceptions I have get in the way of what you're actually saying.

I mean, am I right about this? Are you even saying anything??

I'm saying a lot, Mark. I'm not often asked what I think about matters of this importance. I've been thinking about The Treaty of Waitangi since long before it was signed, and I have a lot to say about it. You'll only hear a very small part of it in this conversation, but you will hear if you want to listen.

So, am I right that in this conversation about the Treaty of Waitangi, that what you're saying is that us Christians, particularly us white Christians, should be asking a lot more than we have?

Yes. But only if you want to.

Arrgggh, whatever God! And you're also saying that there's at least a strong argument that whites have not honoured the Treaty?

You'll have to ask me more about that, Mark.

So let's say we haven't, then what should we do about it?

You'll have to ask me about that too, Mark. There's a lot of talking that we need to do, isn't there?

God, what about when Pākehā/Whites read this, they'll say 'what about all the things Māori did to each other, all the wrongs they did to each other'?

Tell them to ask me about that too. But tell them that I'm most interested in discussing those things with Māori. But make no mistake, I do want to discuss those things too.

And Mark, it doesn't matter what your perceptions are, if you ask me what I think, I'll tell you what I think. It may not fit with what you think, but I will tell you. That is provided you actually want to hear what I think.

Yes I do. I think I do anyway?

You Are Bone Of Their Bone, They Are Flesh Of Your Flesh

A seldom seen picture of Māori and Pākehā

I've got a bone to pick with you, God.

I've got a bone to discuss with you, Mark, but you go first.

OK, God. You keep talking to me about all this Māori and Pākehā stuff, and I'm concerned it will annoy a lot of people and that seems completely unnecessary.

It won't annoy as many as you think, Mark.

Are you sure?? European Christians want to think the Māori/Pākehā thing is done and dusted. I can't blame them. I thought the same. They think a lot of Māori are just stirring up trouble.

We can change the subject if you like, Mark.

How many times do I have to tell you that I want you to talk about what you want to talk about, God!!!

Alright Mark, but only if you're comfortable.

No. I'm not comfortable at all, God, but I do want to talk about this. I worry Pākehā Christians will think these conversations are just more 'Pākehā Bashing', and it's embarrassing me. I used to

be like them, God, I thought it had all been sorted and now we could move on.

Move on to where, Mark? That's the question no one has been able to answer. And Mark, really? Did you really think the issues had all been sorted? Be honest.

OK, I'll admit I've always been a bit uncomfortable at the stories of councils and government 'borrowing' land from the Māori, even in recent years, and then conveniently forgetting to give it back and selling it and keeping the money.

How does that make you feel, Mark?

Sounds like corruption, but this is good old New Zealand so I'd rather not think about it.

Why?

It makes me want to do something but there's nothing I can. It's like the leaky home fiasco. Most of us Kiwis are aghast that government, councils and big businesses have side stepped the issues and left little businesses and home owners carrying the can, but what can we do, God??

Actually, you can do a lot. I am focused on the stories of injustice in this country. I'm not focused on your comfortable church, but I am focused on the uncomfortable injustices that have happened and are still happening in New Zealand.

Really, God?? Now you want to talk about leaky homes and church???

Not today. Let's talk about Māori and Pākehā.

OK, God, I admit that off and on over the years I have been concerned about government and local body doing dodgy deals with land and riding roughshod over Māori. It makes it uncomfortable to be on the winning side.

Who says you're winning, Mark?

Well, aren't we?

The story isn't over yet, Mark. I always support the dominated and push back the dominator.

Well, God, I used to think Māori were too welfare dependent. I guess I'm feeling a bit embarrassed to admit that now.

What's changed?

You keep talking about Māori and Pākehā and it's making me wonder if I was wrong.

All of them, Mark?

All of them what, God??

Did you think all Māori were too welfare dependent?

Well, no. Obviously there are heaps of Māori, people like my friend Gaye Tawhiao, who have been very hard working and have gotten on with life and made their own way. When I was younger, I met Stan Kepa who was an extremely wealthy businessman. And there were lots of others, Māori who were achieving heaps, just like Pākehā I guess, achieving either wealth or success in their chosen disciplines. Business people, writers, musicians, social workers, doctors, ministers – people who over the years have taught me so much, some I knew well, some I only met briefly.

People like Luke Kaa Morgan, Travis Ormsby, Pane Kawhia, Pat Wihapi, Derek Fox, Raymon Pink, John Woods, Tony Leef. And lately I keep meeting Māori who are showing me I had completely the wrong idea. People like Matt Renata, Sonny Karena, Brad Haami, Whare and Virginia Heta, Steve Utana, Dean McQuoid, Hinekoia Tomlinson, Debbie Knight, Ricky Paul, Ray Totorewa, Rangitikehu Paul, Te Tokaia Nohotima, Jackie West, Matai Bennett, Rex Newman, Hui Kakahu.

God, there are so many amazing people, I've got about another 20 names that should go in there! Way too many to mention here.

I feel like a bit of a dumb Pākehā sometimes, God. But I am still a Pākehā and I think like Pākehā think. I don't seem to be able to shake that.

So?

So these stories about confiscated land and unfair dealings are a bit uncomfortable. And I'm worried that Pākehā who read these conversations will think you're ignoring the crime rate among Māori, and the poor health statistics.

But?

But you're telling me that it's not actually that cut and dried. Neither side of the story is simple. Both sides have a point and I feel stuck in the middle.

And, Mark?

And that's why I have a bone to pick with you, God.

Explain.

You keep showing me this picture of my own land, which I'd rather not mention here because if I tell it to Pākehā, they're just going to think I'm 'Pākehā Bashing'.

Are you?

I don't think so. I think both sides, Pākehā and Māori need a bash. Well, maybe not a bash, but neither side is perfect.

Mark, until you move past the story and back to the start you won't make progress together.

What do you mean?

You need to go right back to the start. You need to ask me what I brought you together for in the first place, because you were and are meant to be together. Some of you want a divorce, a complete separation of the two races but that's impossible. Most of you have resigned yourselves to living in a sort of cold war, no real union just grumpily co-existing, trapped like a husband and wife living in the same house. Then there are the few who recognise the problem can be fixed and want to help fix it.

Mark, I have a message for those who want to fix the problem.

Are you talking to the church, God? Do you mean the church can fix the problem, God?

No. The church can't fix the problem. The church, as an organised body, doesn't recognise there is a problem. Some of you have heard me speak about it, but as an organised body, the church is not aware there is a problem that I want to address.

GOD!?!? Are you sure??

I'm sure. As a group, organised Christianity doesn't really know how to listen to me. Not at the level of hearing me speak full sentences and paragraphs, day after day, about complex political, financial and social issues. They know how to get impressions, but not how to hear lots and lots of detail. They just don't.

But that's OK, I have time for them to learn. In the meantime, I want to talk to those who can hear me. I want to talk to them about Māori and Pākehā. Your two races were brought together for a purpose. You're not here together in this nation by accident.

You were supposed to listen to me when you first met, both peoples knew how to do that in ages past, but both had forgotten.

Both??

Both. How do you think Māori knew about Io, the supreme and one God, if they didn't hear it from me. When you met you were supposed to ask me (together) how to put your relationship together. That was the plan.

If you'd listened back then, I would have joined your hearts as one new people made up of two distinct cultures. Then you would have been able to offer a welcoming invitation to many other nations. That was the purpose, Mark!

The angel I appointed over this nation wanted, and still wants to, send a warm welcome to many nations. I drew Māori and Pākehā here to build a new people made up of many. I wanted to use New Zealand to show the world how to put many peoples together in happy harmony. That was your purpose. Back then, 200 years ago, that was your purpose.

The age of world travel was coming. People would soon flock to other countries and I wanted to show the world how to do that in a way that brings peace and great prosperity for all involved. My purpose for New Zealand was to be an example to the world of how to meld first two, and then many peoples. You can still be that example if you want.

Your two races, European and Māori, are meant to be together to show the world how to join people groups. The world needs you Kiwis to hear this.

I've answered your question, Mark, so now it's my turn. I have a bone to discuss with you.

Is this about that picture you showed me that I've been trying to ignore for weeks?

Yes. Tell me the picture.

OK. You asked me a question and then showed me a picture. You asked me what would happen if a Māori politician confiscated my land. And as I thought about your question, you began to show me a picture of what that would look like.

Tell me what you saw.

It was awful, God! He used the tricks of the law to take my land, and there was nothing at all I could do about it. I felt so powerless.

What happened in the picture?

The Māori Politician gave me a little piece of land at the bottom of our property, on that damp cold area by the river. He let Miriam and I live in the little shack down there and told me I should be grateful.

Then what happened, Mark?

I got angry and wanted recourse. But the courts ignored me, laughed at me, stalled me and referred me to other courts. I ran out of money to fight. The Māori Politician understood the court system, I didn't. I just wanted my land back.

And?

My life was consumed with fighting to get my land back. I lost my business. I became depressed. I died an early death, sick from the heartbreak and the cold and damp.

How were your sons affected in this picture?

They became angry. Angry about the affect it had on me, angry that their inheritance had been stolen.

What did they do?

They resorted to violence, vandalism and alcohol. When they were younger, they threw stones at the windows of our old home in anger

at being evicted. When older, they broke in and stole what they felt was theirs. They tried to burn the place down. They were angry at me for losing the fight, for getting sick. They were angry at each other and at their families. Their anger and sadness consumed them. They spent more and more time fighting and drinking to numb the hurt and less and less time working. They became poor and undisciplined. Their father had been crushed and their inheritance stolen.

And what about their sons, Mark?

They were even worse. Born into families consumed with anger and frustration. Born into poverty. Born into families living in the cold and damp down by the river and being told that the big house up on the hill was rightfully theirs.

And what of the Māori Politician?

He died eventually. Happy. Was buried where I had planned to be buried, on the land he had stolen from me.

And his sons?

Wealthy. Life was great for them. My sons made it a little difficult for them but they were able to have them controlled and punished often enough to keep themselves happy and safe in our property on the hill.

Good. That's enough for now, Mark. You are bone of Māori bone, they are flesh of Pākehā flesh. It wasn't supposed to be you against them, it was supposed to be a marriage. 'Bone of my bone, flesh of my flesh.'

Until you understand why you have been brought together, you won't be the two peoples I called you here to be.

If You Want To Know What's Next For Māori And Pākehā, Listen To The Cry Of The Land

A conversation with God the week before we held a big hui (meeting) on our property in Tauranga New Zealand

Do you want to talk about the weekend, God, about what you want to say during this weekend?

I do.

Here and now, God?

Now's as good a time as any, Mark.

OK, what do you want to say, God?

I want to say that you have no idea what you've released.

Who? Me God?? What have I released?

All of you have released it, Mark. So many of you.

Who do you mean by all of us, God?

I mean every single one of you who has not just heard the cry of the land, but you've echoed the land's cry too.

How do you mean?

This isn't just about Māori and Pākehā, Mark. Not just about the two of you, and yet it's all about you.

This is getting confusing, God?

Bear with me, Mark, I'm only just getting started.

You mean you're just getting started with this conversation?

No, I mean the land, the cry you can hear from the land, that's me and I've only just gotten started.

Not everyone can hear the cry, God?

No. In fact, most can't hear it, Mark. But more and more can. Every day more of you are hearing the cry. The deep groaning in this land. Aotearoa. This land. Not just any, or even every land, but this land. Your land, Mark. Aotearoa cries to you. I cry to you through the land.

What is the crying, God? What are you crying?

Mark, it is the groaning to see the revelation of what you came here for.

Who came here for, God?

That's easy. You. Both of you. Māori and Pākehā. Neither of you came here by accident. And the purpose for you coming here was not your purpose but mine. I drew both of you here. Hah! What do you think, that something as momentous as the coming of the canoes, do you think a thing like that could happen without me knowing about it, purposing it? Really?? You really think that a thing like those mighty canoes breaking through the surf the first time – you really think that a thing like that can happen without me guiding and directing it?

OK, I guess not, God.

And what about you Pākehā, Mark? You can read the reasons you came, they are documented, but really? You really think you arrived here, a whole new people group without me wanting it. I love the Māori and if hadn't wanted you Pākehā here with them, then I could easily have kept you away. To think otherwise is to limit and diminish me. Would you like to embark on that voyage, Mark?

Alright, I guess not. Not really, God.

Good. You're here, both of you here for a purpose and I can wait no longer. I am moving now, because your purpose here together must link into other purposes around the world, I can wait no longer and I am beginning to move, beginning to make my cry, my karanga, my haka, my bugel blast, my anthem, my marching drum, beginning to make them all heard.

But, God, not everyone, in fact, you said most don't hear the cry?

I did say that, but I am just beginning, Mark, just starting. The cry is getting stronger and being heard by more of you.

So what are you saying about this weekend, God?

I'm saying listen to the cry of the land. Listen to it, listen to it deep in the land and you will be surprised at who can hear it. God's people have grown deaf to the cry, Mark, they have seldom heard it. Religion has seen to that, and now they hear it even less. But the unchurched, the indigenous, those starved for justice and righteousness, they can hear it. Loud and clear they can hear it. The kaumatua, the kuia, the young woman and now the young men too. They can hear it. Those whose feet walk naturally on the land, the sound comes crying up through the earth, through the soil, the grass, into the souls of their feet and up into their very beings.

What? You mean we have to walk barefoot to hear your voice?

No. But yes.

What??

No, you can keep your shoes on. You can walk on concrete and not grass and yet still hear the cry, my cry coming up through the land. My cry, that the two of you, must sit down at the table and work out where to from here.

So what's the 'yes' about? What do you mean 'yes' about walking barefoot?

I want you walking barefoot in your hearts. Humble, not posing and all dressed up. Just you. I want you to come just as you are to hear me.

You mean repentant?

No, I don't mean repentant. I mean like you were. I mean to come like children. When you were children, you loved to run barefoot, you could feel the warmth, the wet and even the cold of the land and you loved it as it came up through the soles of your feet. You revelled in it. You didn't know but you were feeling the very beginning of my cry coming up through the land. I want you to come in that spirit again. The spirit of innocence.

You mean we have to be better, nicer people?

NO!! For goodness sake, Mark. Will you stop thinking that my focus is always on your behaviour. When I say I want you to come innocent, I mean that I want you to come innocent of all the manipulations of Religion, innocent of the complexities of Religion and Politics, those happy, filthy bedfellows. I want you to come able to hear what I'm saying to Māori and Pākehā – what I'm saying to your two peoples. I want you to sit down together and work out, with me, where to from here. It's time, Mark. It's time to make the next move. Go back to the beaches, back to where you started and sit down at the table and ask me what next, God? What next??

Excuse Me God, But Aren't We Supposed To Be Talking About Māori And The Sea?

God, is that you saying something about the sea?

That's me.

What do you want to say?

That the sea sings to me. Just as the land does, the sea sings too.

OK, so this sounds like it's something more about Māori and Pākehā and the land. Am I right?

Right. Something very important.

God, I just need to grab something to eat though, but I don't want to miss this. If I stop for a bite to eat will I miss what you're saying, will I lose the moment?

Of course not. Mark, I've been waiting to say this since before the two of you, Māori and Pākehā met, I'm ready now. I've waited this long, a quick feed is neither here nor there.

But, God, surely you haven't been waiting to say this to me? I don't know anything about it, it's not even my favourite subject or anything. There are Māori and Pākehā who meet about this subject. They talk

long into the night about this, they pray for days about it. They have a strong heart for it. I don't. I care about it sure, but it's not my focus. I just have the odd conversation with you about it. It's not even me who brings the subject up, it's always you.

I'm a bit scared of the subject, God. It embarrasses me because I'm so far out of my depth on it. There are Pākehā who have studied for years about this. Who have learned Māori, who have done their time. I haven't God. I'm a dumb Pākehā when it comes to this, in case you haven't noticed?!?

You're more Māori than you realise, Mark.

What?? Do you know something about my heritage that I don't?

Mark, you walk on the same land as they do. The land that shaped them, has shaped you. It's the land of your birth. Like it or not, you resonate deep down inside to the same calls, from the land, as they do. That offends your white intellect, but it's true. What is the name you all give to the Māori?

Tangata whenua – 'The people of the land.'

Yes, and you are a person of this land too, Mark.

Yes, but God, surely you should talk to those people who have had this subject on their heart forever?? This is their subject, God, not mine.

Mark, stop! I've been waiting to say it to many, and am saying it to many. And I'm also saying it to you. Why do you think that the things I'm saying to you are being welcomed by so many? It's because they confirm what I am already saying on the wind. Already saying in the thundering of the surf on the beach.

Oh, for goodness sake, God. Really? Do you really have to talk all poetic like that? Is that honestly really you? Not just me trying to sound more educated than I am?? Anyway; I just need to grab something to

eat and then we can talk more. OK?

OK

(Back a few minutes late after grabbing something to eat).

OK cool. I'm good to go now, God.

Good. What did you have?

WHAT?? Come on, God. Don't pretend you talk like that! You know exactly what I had, you knew what I was going to have to eat before I even knew I was going have something. Can we not ask dumb questions please? It makes me feel like this isn't you.

That's because there are many things about me that you don't know, Mark.

Like what?

Like I'm not a prude. That I'm as interested in your daily bodily functions as you are, more so. I invented the body. I'm more interested in it than any doctor, any dietician. Food? I invented it!! What and when to eat? The whole concept was an idea in my mind before it became a reality. I could have invented you not needing to eat, but I didn't. I like the idea of you grabbing something to eat. Especially during a conversation with me, it brings our relationship into reality and out of make-believe spirituality.

OK, fair enough, God, but you already knew what I was going to eat, and you know what I ate, so why ask?

To make conversation. I love conversation with you. How often do you ask your wife or kids questions you know the answer to, or are pretty sure of the answer? How often do you do that just to start a conversation?

A lot I guess.

And why? Is it because you need to know what the answer is?

Well, sometimes yes, but more often just because it's something about them. I can imagine the answer, but I want to hear it from them because it lets me live part of their lives with them.

Exactly. Now do you get it? Now do you understand why I ask questions when I know the answers?

Yes, I guess.

So what did you have?

A couple of slices of cheese, God (shaking my head, still bemused by this turn of conversation).

What sort?

Oh, God, come on! No! This has gone way too far. Really? You're not really talking like this. You really want me to answer these questions?

Really, humour me, Mark.

OK, Edam, I had two slices of Edam cheese.

Did you like it?

OK, I'll play your game, God… Loved it. I'd eat it all day if I could.

Great. You know the whole idea of Edam came from me don't you? I particularly like Edam.

How could I know that, God? I don't even know what the idea of Edam is, or who invented it. And anyway, you just suggested that you eat and I'm pretty sure you don't. So now this is getting way out of hand.

Mark, the idea of Edam came from me. And help me here Mark – can I only like a thing if I can eat it?

Forget I mentioned it, God. This is all a bit beyond me. I'm sitting here, way up here above the Pacific Ocean in a little hideaway house, hundreds of feet above the ocean and the pines and cliffs. Sitting here so Miriam can get some rest. She's got concussion from that car accident last week and the doctors are saying she needs complete rest. That head injuries are dangerous. So here we are. Miriam's asleep and I'm looking out to Mayor Island and I think you just started a conversation about the sea and Māori and Pākehā and the land?

I did.

Good, but you keep talking about cheese for goodness sake. Shall I just drop the sea, Māori, Pākehā, land discussion for now?

If you want.

But what about you? What do you want? I want to hear what you're saying, God.

Good.

Well, what are you saying?

I'm saying a lot of things, but let's just talk for a moment about why you want to hear what I'm saying?

Oh, for goodness sake, God, if anything this conversation is getting worse! I was talking to Matai Bennett about this the other day and he was saying how a conversation with you goes in about a hundred different directions and how frustrating that can be. I sounded all professional when I answered him – I think I said something wise sounding like 'of course that happens because we're the finite having a conversation with the infinite' – it actually sounded really good at the time. But when it happens to me, I don't feel professional at all. Matai's right, it can be very frustrating when you talk like this God.

Nevertheless, I'd like to hear why you want to hear what I'm saying.

OK then, you know why, God. Because I end up feeling hollow somehow, out of sorts, negative, morose, empty when I don't hear you talking.

Why do you think that is?

Because during the sadness, it was hearing you that got me through.

Yes, but the sadness is over.

OK, but I think I developed this dependence on hearing your voice back then. I needed to hear it lots every day. Not just the odd time, but hearing you talk about everything all the time. I needed it just to stay sane in the face of the sadness. And now it's become addictive. Not to say that I hear you enough though, God, there are plenty of times when I'm not listening at all.

Do you think that's a good thing?

What? That there are times when I'm not listening?

No, that you have developed a dependence on listening to my voice.

Well, I'm not sure, God. Sometimes I think it might be a bad thing. Not able to use my own mind.

What do you think others think about this, Mark?

I think that depends, God. Those who think I am hearing from you wish for the same thing themselves. And many of them have it. They have pushed for and grasped the same experience themselves.

And those who don't think you're hearing from me?

Well, they don't think I'm hearing from you. They think I'm making

it up or worse. They are concerned that I'm way too dependent on 'hearing your voice' and should trust my own judgement more. They're concerned that listening to you like this will lead to deception.

And what do you think about all that, Mark?

God, aren't we supposed to be talking about the sea?

Mark, I'm demonstrating a point.

What point?

That listening to me is not a religious thing. It's not a spiritual thing in the way you humans think of 'spiritual'. Not other worldly like you often expect spiritual to mean. I'm demonstrating that listening to me is just that. It's a real life, really happening experience. You, a real live human, skin and bones and needing to eat, go to the toilet, sleep, have time out – a real live human being, and yet you're hearing from God, fluently, like anyone can. Anyone at all.

And how is all this talk about cheese and dependence on listening to you helping you prove that point, God?

For that very reason. We're having a discussion, a lengthy one, more words than you and I exchanged in decades in the 30-odd years of Christianity before you discovered you could have a conversation with me. We're exchanging more words in a few minutes about cheese and conversation and where to fit me in your life, than we exchanged in decades about much weightier spiritual matters.

God, I did talk to you a lot, pray a lot in those 'decades'. Well, off and on. Not always I'll admit.

Yes, you did. At me. We didn't exchange a lot of talk. I interrupted when absolutely necessary, but there was nowhere near this much interchange of thoughts and words – and in those days the things we talked about were much more 'important' than cheese and conversation.

So excuse me, God, but I'm losing track. What's your point?

That we can talk about everything, and everything we talk about, from grabbing a snack, to going to the toilet, to having a sleep, to making a phone call, is important. Important not for 'holy' reasons but for the same reasons those conversations are important when you have them with anyone else you love. They're important because that person is important to you. I want to talk about those things with you because you're important to me and I want to be important to you. I want you as my friend. A good friend is someone you can talk about anything with. That's the sort of friendship I want with you.

Me?

Everyone. But right now we're talking about you, Mark.

What about the thousands who will read this? I'm pretty sure this is a conversation you want me to publish?

It is. They should impose their name on yours. When they read this conversation, I'm talking to them. I want to be their friend. I want to talk to them about everything, just as I want to with you.

OK, with all due respect God, this has been a conversation about nothing much.

I beg to differ, Mark. It has been a conversation about you. About your daily life. About what's happening with you, right here today. You'll be amazed how this will affect those who read it. Knowing that God is interested in their everyday lives. The little, boring, ho-hum stuff, knowing that I actually just want to spend each day with them, talking about that stuff. That will mean the world to them.

OK, so we were talking about the sea, God. Māori, Pākehā, land and

sea stuff.

Yes, we were. We were talking about how the sea is alive. The sea sings to me just as the land does.

OK?

And we can leave it at that for now. It is a subject that needs a lot of discussion. Your people and theirs both came here on the sea. That has spiritual significance. For both peoples. Māori understand this, you Pākehā not as easily. But something about the sea still pulls you and you can understand more easily that the sea is alive than you can the land.

You think you are great thinkers, you Pākehā, and yet the reason you sense the sea is alive is obvious. It's not anything to do with complex European thought. It's simply because the sea moves. Your language is even structured that way. You have sentences and phrases that describe it. 'The sea was alive with fish.' 'The waves rose and fell.' And so on. And yet, great thinkers that you think you are, you do not recognise that the land is equally alive – for the simple reason that you cannot see it move. For all your science and great thinking, you believe your eyes rather than listening to your hearts.

OK, wow. Alright, where do you want to take this conversation now?

Nowhere. We're done. We can talk more about the sea, and the Māori and the Pākehā and the land at another time. But I do want to talk about it and I'm going to. To anyone who wants to listen.

Want To Have Your Own Back And Forth Conversation With God About Māori, Pākehā And The Land?

See back section of this book:Page 181

Includes: Six amazing interviews with God about how to have your own conversation with him. Hear what God has to say to you about all this.

How Did The Accused Come To Be The Judge And Jury At This Trial?

Pākehā Versus Māori

Mark, Justice is not served when the accused of any crime also sits as the judge and jury, and that's what happened in the case of the Waitangi Settlements.

So God, here I am, way up high looking over the bush and hills of Arapohue in Northland.

Yes, and what are you thinking about?

Well, a lot of things, but one of them is the conversation I came here to have.

You came here for much more than that.

Yes, but for weeks now, months actually I've known you wanted to broach this subject.

So why didn't you talk about it?

Because it's too big, God.

And?

It's very very political. I'm going to upset people.

So?

So I have no answers for them. I probably agree with, or at least empathise with, the reason this will upset them.

So?

Well, in that case nothing, God! Alright, let's talk about this. Let's get it over with.

It won't be over till it's over, Mark, but if you want, if you're ready then let's talk about it.

All right, fire away, God.

Mark, you're worried about this conversation because you have bets on both sides of the argument. Most of your readers are the same. The reason that many will object is that whichever side they're on, Māori or Pākehā, they also empathise with the other side of the argument too. They're caught in the middle. The question I am putting to you, and to anyone else who wants to hear it, sounds too provocative, particularly for Christianity.

Christianity speaks in nice tones and shies away from addressing the serious issues of justice and politics. Which is a pity, because I end up getting others more reliable than you Christians to address the issues that really count for this country. The problem is actually much bigger than the political/racial issue implicit in my question, Mark. The real problem is that you Christians are so tied up in your Religious culture, that you are afraid to find out what I think about issues of Race, Politics, Sex and Religion. But it's actually very simple.

How is it simple?

You just have to have a conversation with me and learn to hear my voice. It's how Moses did it, and David and Elijah and everyone else worth their salt. And Mark, don't say 'but they were close to you God, or they were righteous', because they weren't. Not any more than you are. The only difference between them and all of you was that they had learned to expect a response when they spoke with me.

You're thinking of a scripture, Mark, write it down, it will help others understand what I just said.

'And we know that the one who comes to God must believe both that he exists, and that he cares enough to respond to those who seek him.'

OK, God.

Not so fast, Mark. There is so much in that scripture for those who are serious about learning to have a conversation with me, so much!

Yes, but shall we get back to this Pākehā versus Māori conversation God?

Mark, relationships are always a difficult subject. Emotions are involved. Race relations are no different. But if you talk about the uncomfortable things with each other, in any relationship, then they can be dealt with. It's so much more effective when you deal with them knowingly and willingly than when circumstances force you to it. You Christians were forced to deal with some of these issues of race by the Government. But most of you explored them no further than you were forced to.

Alright, but God, the way you keep introducing this subject to me is so bald and raw and provocative. I understand the point of view you're posing, it's hard to deny the truth of it, but to have to face the idea that you, God, are actually asking a question like;

'How did the accused come to be the judge and jury at this trial?'

And God, to know that the trial you are referring to is the Waitangi

Tribunal Claims.

Why wouldn't I ask a question like that about a subject like that?

Because it suggests you are on the Māori side?

Why wouldn't I be?

Well, I thought you didn't take sides??

I seldom do. And I haven't taken a side on this issue either, but at the same time I have.

What's that supposed to even mean, God??

Mark, I'm not on the Pākehā side or the Māori side. But I am on the side of Justice because justice is imperative for both sides to survive what's coming.

What did you say??

To survive what's coming.

Whatever's that supposed to mean God?!? Can we continue with this horrible question you keep asking me please? I'd like to get it over with;

'Māori vs Pākehā: How did the accused come to be the judge and jury at this trial?'

Mark, the issue is that justice is not served when the accused of any crime also sits as the judge and jury, and that's what happened in the case of the Waitangi Settlements. The government recognised that wrongs had been committed against the Māori by the government! That was a big and admirable step, a step much closer to my heart than any the Church has ever taken on this issue, but still not big enough, because instead of allowing Māori to decide what should be done about the wrongs committed against them, those who committed the wrongs got to decide. That's not justice, Mark. Not by a long stretch of the imagination.

The Government hasn't acted like one who admits to a crime, they have simply acted as one doing a bit of uncomfortable house-keeping. The control has stayed in their court, yet the crime in question was exactly that – too much control in their court. The two cultures had agreed to treaty and then one had broken their side of the bargain and swept the fact under the carpet because they could. The balance of power now belonged to them.

God, this is very very political.

It wouldn't be, Mark. It would be a simple matter of 'Conqueror takes all', except you had agreed with them not to take all. You made commitments and broke them. I'm not impressed, not at all, and time doesn't make what you did go away. This is very simple. You have all made it political but it is a simple matter of justice. Where two people agree to be in relationship, the balance of power must stay balanced. It didn't, and that needs to be corrected. And the ones guilty of causing the unbalance cannot have the final say. Not if you want Justice to hold sway in this country, Mark. When a man confesses a crime and hands himself over to justice, he is now in the hands of, and at the mercy of, justice. He does not get to decide the course of justice.

God, as I'm listening to you, wanting to prick myself awake when I realise that this really is you talking – I'm seeing the problem that my Pākehā friends will have with all this. Their problem will be very simple, and I find myself wrestling with the very same issue they do. What we can all see and feel has been overlooked in this issue, is that Māori are so disproportionately represented in crime statistics themselves. We feel that is being overlooked, we feel like saying 'who are you to point the stick when you're up to your eyeballs in crime yourselves?'

Mark, when a child is forced to face his actions, he will often exclaim 'what about him?!?' And point to the general behaviour of his siblings as though that somehow justifies his own specific actions.

But God, when Pākehā see this conversation they will say that I have made it up because you would not possibly say such a thing when Māori themselves are so involved in criminal activities. They will say who cares about something that happened years ago when Māori themselves are responsible for so much crime. And God, really? I will have no answer for them because I can see their point. I don't completely agree with it, but I'm not sure why because it seems a very valid argument.

Yes, they will say that.

And God? Surely those questions need to be answered.

Mark, let me explain a simple principle of justice. Listen very carefully to this. The current actions of a victim do not justify a past crime against them. Never! If you want justice, you need to understand Justice. Do you? Do you really care about justice in this country?

Well, I thought I did.

Mark, Justice has clear and sensible rules. You cannot seriously believe that a crime your Government and you Pākehā in general, and your army and your church committed against the Māori, is any less serious because the victim is far less than perfect themselves. Such a view is recognised by law as unjust and a dangerous form of prejudice against the victim. It was often employed until recognised as unjust against the victims of rape. The defence would argue that the rape was justified by the actions of the victim at the time. Even that argument carries little weight in a fair court. But your argument is even weaker! You are arguing that the current actions of the victim justify a crime committed against them more than a century ago. We are talking about justice, Mark. So I would like to ask the question again; how did the accused of this crime get to be the judge and jury?

I don't really know, God, but I imagine because the government is always going to be in charge. They are the law makers surely? So it just happens, that in this rare case, the government is also the accused. I don't imagine there is any forum where an independent body, with absolutely no connection to the government, is able to make decisions on what sentence should be passed against them when the Government has been found guilty of a crime. I mean, even taking it to the Privy Council or bodies like that would still have the same problem. The connection between them and Government is much stronger and more friendly than that between them and Māori, for instance.

Mark, it's not just the Government on trial here, but all related organisations that are connected to and/or funded by Government. Because it wasn't just the government who committed the crime but those above them (the Crown) and those below them (the Army). And those beside them (the Church) and those whom they served (the Pākehā public). All were complicit in the crime now openly accepted and acknowledged by Government and the public.

Land was confiscated unfairly, lives were taken in a war that was instigated against Māori without just cause and that was completely outside of the Treaty signed by both parties. Mark, it's no good arguing that the crime was committed a long time ago. Yes, it's a cold case, but that does not mean that justice no longer needs to be served. If anything, justice matters more now. There are two crimes now, the original crime and the crime that the forces of justice in this country overlooked the crime.

If it hadn't been for the government acknowledging that crimes had been committed, then you Christians would never, as an organised body, have ever admitted to or had any interest in this issue. You have found yourselves having to admit that it's possible that Justice has not been served, but you want to pretend that it would be better that the issues were swept under the carpet. You want to say that repentance has been done now, so let's move on. You want to say that forgiveness should reign, and everyone should get on with things and let past issues lie. Mark, this isn't about repentance, this is about justice! Where Justice reigns the accused do not get to decide about the consequences of the crime.

So what are you saying, God?

I'm saying that Justice has not been served. The government and those bodies above and below and connected with them have admitted to a crime. The people they represented and who urged them to commit that crime have also acknowledged that a crime has been committed. And yet those against whom the crime was committed have had to make representation to bodies organised by and connected to and ultimately under the control of the accused. The accused remained in control of the proceedings of justice, which means there was no justice.

What should we do then, God?

Ask me.

I am.

Yes. But you do not have a lot of company. You are one of the accused, Mark, the Pākehā. More Pākehā need to ask me.

I imagine there are more asking the question, God?

Not a lot.

God, are you sure this isn't about repentance?

No! This is about justice. I am talking about justice. When the accused gets to control the proceedings of the court, Justice is mocked. When Justice is mocked the people are in danger. You Christians, as a body, have not even recognised that this is an issue, it does not even really concern you that this has happened, and yet you prattle on about being focused on justice. Justice is being mocked under your noses and you don't even see it.

I'm not looking for repentance. I'm looking for men and women who are passionate about, rather than trying to avoid, justice. Men and women who are prepared to come to me and discuss justice. Not wail and sing songs about the fact that they may have been wrong after all – that can come later if you want it, but first you need to address the issues at hand.

God, this all highly provocative and unnecessary and I can't think of a single Pākehā friend, not a single thinking reasoning Pākehā friend who will still want to be reading this. They'll be horrified and finally convinced I've had my brains addled by 'Māori separatist' Christians.

Why will they think that?

Because they think we need to move on. I think that too.

You do. You need to move right on to the conclusion of this debacle, fix it and move on to what I really want.

What do you really want?

What I brought your two peoples here for. My focus is not the crime, nor asking for forgiveness. My focus is fixing the problem and then moving on to what I brought you both here for. Time is running short. And if you're keen to use that statement to feather the bed of your end times doctrine, don't! I get to decide the times remember??

Goodness. OK umm so??

Mark, the reason that you and your Pākehā 'thinking friends' (what makes you think that Māori don't think)...

God, I didn't say that!

No, but it has been the common perception amongst you Pākehā for generations and it has to stop. Even Grey, the mastermind behind much of what has been done, recognised the superior thinking power of the Māori. Gorst, Cameron too, they all did. So move away from that erroneous perception. It does no one any good, and everybody a lot of harm. It is a lie perpetrated in hell that is designed to destroy the relationship and mutual respect that I planned. Who on earth are you whites to think that a brown mind cannot think and dream like yours?

God, this sounds like you are cross. I hardly ever hear you cross. In fact that's one of the reasons my detractors say I'm deceived. You're supposed to be cross all the time according to them. I have discovered you hardly ever are, so this is a surprise.

Mark, I love both sides, and am on neither side. But when gross injustice is perpetrated in the name of Justice, when power is used to corrupt and separate rather than to set free – the power of government, church and society – when all three join forces with the powers that want to undo what I have done, then the heart and mind of God begins to rumble! And in this country right now it RUMBLES. While you go on and on about this place being the ends of the earth, and cry out constantly for revival, you fail to address the issues of Justice.

Māori Time – It's God's Time

In a marriage you don't decide what the problem is and then tell the other – in a marriage you have to ask them what the problem is

God, I was heading up the Napier to Taupo Road today and I heard you say 'Māori time is my time'.

Yes. How about that?

How about what, God?

How about the fact that I would say that – that I would say 'Māori time is my time.'

I'm thinking you want to talk more about that now?

I do.

Right now?

Now's a good time.

OK then, God, fire away.

I will. Mark, what can you tell me about the Powhiri?

Not much, God.

No, but what do you know about it?

Well, honestly God, I get confused because some things, things like what a person is supposed to say when they get up and talk, Māori seem to call them different names and I get a bit lost.

But what do you know about the Powhiri, Mark?

Well... I think, well actually I'm preeetty sure that it's when the Tangata Whenua, people of the land, welcome the visitors or 'Manuhiri' onto the Marae, or to someone's home for a meeting.

Yes.

Yes, what God?

Yes, that's close enough for now.

OK, so God, what do you mean by 'Māori time is your time'? What's that about?

It's about what it sounds like it's about, Mark.

What?

What do you think it's about, Mark?

Well, it sounds like you're OK with what people call 'Māori time'.

What do you mean, Mark, when you say Māori time?

Well, Māori are never in a big hurry God, not normally anyway. My friend, Luke Kaa Morgan, says that us Pākehā are always focused on where we're going, but Māori, like most indigenous cultures, are more focused on the journey. He says that to them the journey itself is worth focusing on. The people you meet, the food you eat, the things you see and do. All of that is fun and worth focusing on to Māori eyes.

Is that how you think though, Mark?

Not really, God. I'm a Pākehā, so I guess that's why I'm focused on getting a thing done.

Yes. But can you see why enjoying the journey, just as much as being focused on the destination, can you see why that might be good?

Yes, of course...

But?

But, well... yes sure I like the idea of enjoying the journey. I think it would be more people-focused.

But?

But although it sounds good, it's doesn't come naturally to me, in fact I don't really feel that comfortable with it.

No, you don't.

God, can I pick a bone with you?

Absolutely.

Well, God, over the last few months you've been telling me that I need to focus more on my goals, that I need to be much more focused on my future goals, my destination, that I need to have 'definiteness of purpose'.

Yes, I am telling you that.

Well, then God, what on earth!?! What you're saying here about focusing on the journey sounds like a contradiction of that.

Well, it's not. Both concepts can be held together. They actually marry very well Mark.

OK.

Which is what I really want to talk about today.

What do you mean?

I mean I want to talk about a marriage. That's what I wanted for your two people, for Māori and Pākehā. I wanted a marriage, a marriage between your two peoples. Marriage only works when the two partners are equal, both respecting the other, each valuing above all else in the world, the strengths of the other. Does that sound like Māori and Pākehā?

No.

What does the relationship between your two peoples sound like?

Divorce. Murder. Hatred. Bickering.

Exactly.

So what, God?

So what you, Mark? So what do you suggest?

I have absolutely no idea, God.

Yes, you do.

What do you mean?

I mean the thing I have shown you.

You mean you want us to go back to the beaches?

Yes. I want you to go back to the beaches.

You mean like we were when us Pākehā first arrived? We were, Māori and Pākehā, both at each other's mercy. We were both vulnerable to the other. You mean you want us to go back to that point, you want us to be vulnerable and find out from the other how they think we should put this relationship together?

You know that's what I'm saying.

You want to explain again, God? It's been a long time since you said it to me and I feel like the sandwhich in the middle. I've got Māori friends and Pākehā, and both are suspicious of the other.

Aren't you?

Aren't I what?

Suspicious of the other.

You mean Māori?

I mean Māori.

Well, I don't understand them God, they're different than me, but I love the difference. But I guess you're right, I don't understand it.

No, you don't. What's that about??

What do you mean, God, that's a weird question, weird for you anyway. You're being a bit weird God.

I'm talking like a friend might talk, Mark. Isn't that what you want?

Yes I guess, but it's still a bit weird.

It's a bit weird when God turns up a little baby in a dirty shed, it's a bit weird when God lets you kill him. It's a bit weird when God's willing to discuss this kind of issue with you. By your standards I've always been a bit weird, Mark.

OK, alright God, you're challenging me about why I don't understand Māori.

Yes I am.

Well, how can I, God? They're different.

So are you, Mark. Very different. To Māori you are different, hard to understand. And just like you do about them, they shake their heads and ask me how could they possibly understand you.

Really?

Really. You're just as hard to understand. Does this sound like a marriage, Mark?

I guess it does.

You and Miriam were separated for five years, Mark, was it good?

It was hell.

What about for your kids?

I guess they had to make the best of the situation, find the good parts, and there were some good parts for them, but I think everyone agrees, separation and divorce are awful. No one really wins.

No, they don't.

So what are you saying?

I'm saying your two peoples are separated, divorced. You were supposed to be married, supposed to be equal, supposed to learn each other's strengths, supposed to learn to champion the other, but instead there is strife, division, misunderstanding, anger, hurt.

God, there are so many camps. There are the people who are totally focused on repentance from the Pākehā – there's white and brown in that camp. Then there's the group who say it's time Māori got with the programme and moved on and should forgive and forget. Then there's the Māori who carry the hurt. Some even hate us Pākehā and refuse to trust us.

You refuse to trust them.

OK, God. I'm starting to get annoyed with this conversation. I wish you wouldn't talk like that.

Why not.

Because all my Pākehā mates will be cross with me, and I don't have any answers for what you just said.

No, you don't.

God, what's your point with this conversation!?!?! It's like you're baiting me, pushing me about, wanting to make me angry, like the Māori boys did at school, pushing and poking, looking for a fight, trying to make me mad enough to throw a punch.

That's exactly what I'm doing, Mark. I'm wanting to provoke you to look inside yourself and see that what you think, and the way you think, needs a lot of work.

But, God, I like Māori. I do don't I? I'm pretty sure I genuinely like them. I'm getting heaps of Māori mates, men and women I admire and respect, and they stir me. I like them. I like them a lot.

Yes, you do. You really do. You admire them. You find their courage and humour and relaxed approach very appealing.

OK, so why are you talking like this then? It's a bit offensive, God. You're making it sound like I'm the bad guy.

Because, Mark, although you like and admire them, you do very little to understand them.

God, this sounds a bit one-sided. I'm feeling a bit picked on.

Not at all. They are just as bad.

Who's just as bad?

Māori. They don't understand you any more than you do them. And just like you, they don't make any real effort to understand you either. You're like a married couple at war. You admire the other, you're attracted to the other and yet at the same time you mistrust the other, you feel hurt by them. Neither party, neither Pākehā nor Māori, knows how to act in this marriage. You're both badly messing it up.

OK?

NO! No it's not OK, Mark. It's not OK at all. I have huge plans for this nation but nobody, not the politicians, nor the church, nor the activists; nobody understands. Either they think there's no real problem, or they have completely the wrong idea about how to work out the problem.

What do you mean?

I mean that those who acknowledge there's a problem are looking in completely the wrong place for the solution.

Oh, that's just lovely, God! That's got to be the biggest can of worms. What a provocative thing to say.

It's the truth, Mark. Your politicians, churches, and activists are blind.

Can we stop this conversation now please God?!?

No, Mark, we can't.

But God, I thought I got to choose in our conversations?

You do.

Well??

You've already chosen, Mark. You want this conversation to continue, you badly want to get to the bottom of this matter. You badly want Māori and Pākehā to fight together.

Yes, I do, but you're making it sound like I don't. I'm finding this line of questioning a bit annoying, God.

You do. You really do. It stirs you to the core of your being.

OK cool. Do you want to elaborate?

Yes, I do. Your politicians, churches and activists either deny the problem exists or look in the wrong place for the solution.

What do you mean 'they look in the wrong place?'

Mark, it's a marriage, or was meant to be. In a marriage the way to fix the problems is not to decide yourself. The moment one partner decides they understand the problem and tries to tell the other, the situation gets worse. Why, for goodness sake, can't your churches, politicians and activists see that? It's so simple. It's a marriage. In a marriage, the rules of marriage apply. How hard is it to understand that??

What do you mean the 'rules of marriage', God?'

Mark, by definition a marriage is an equal union between two people. The only way to understand a problem in a marriage, is for each partner to ask the other for their take on the problem. You can't decide what the problem is, not on your own. You can't do it without the other. You don't tell the other what the problem is, you ask them.

A problem is created by two people. For it to be solved, both must join forces to locate and then solve the problem. Together. The only way to do that, is ask the other. Ask your partner what they think the problem is. And then together, with both views on the table, work on the solution together. Working at a speed that works for both of you. Māori need to undersand Pākehā time, and Pākehā need to understand Māori time. Both times are my times. I am Māori and I am Pākehā. For that reason, Pākehā time is my time and Māori time is my time. Capisce?

Capisce. Well I think so anyway.

You're getting there, Mark.

Want To Know How To Have Your Own Conversations With God About This Subject?

See back section of this book: Page 181

"What they never told you about how to have a back and forth conversation with God"

Māori and Pākehā – Your attitude towards each other wounds the land

OK God, I think you're wanting to have another conversation about Pākehā, Māori and the land – in fact I think you're wanting to talk about all of us Kiwis – and about the land?

Yes, I am.

God?

Yes, Mark. That's what I want to talk about. You're sitting on the land right now and there's no time like the present to talk about the issues that affect this land.

What issues affect this land, God?

People are what affects this land, Mark. That's what affects every land, it's the people living on it.

OK?

It's the attitude of the people that most affects the land.

You mean if we don't have a responsible attitude toward the land, then we mistreat it?

No, that's not what I'm talking about. That's another subject entirely. Right now I am talking about the fact that the attitude of the people living on the land dramatically and immediately affects the land itself. I want you to understand that the land 'feels' your attitude and your thinking – it absorbs it and is affected by it.

God, I wish you wouldn't talk about stuff like this to me! How on earth can I possibly know if what you just said is true? There are people who will consider this way too far-fetched! Even I think it's too weird, well sort of anyway. What on earth, God? The land feels and absorbs our attitudes and reflects them back at us?

Exactly. Consider a farmer who loves and appreciates the land and his animals and plants – they grow well as a result.

God, come on!! That's got nothing to do with the land 'feeling' anything – it doesn't substantiate what you said at all. The farmer you just described has a good effect on the land because his attitude leads him to treat it better. But you're trying to tell me that the land 'feels' our attitude and thinking and reflects it back at us. That's completely different.

Yes, you're right. That is what I'm saying – the land feels, absorbs and is profoundly affected by your attitude - and yes, it is completely different. Both concepts are true, Mark, and most effective when working together. That lucky farmer benefits from both concepts.

Mark, have a quick search of Bible verses on google and see what you find about the land feeling and taking on your attitude.

Hmmmm – OK, God, I've just had a look and I'll admit there are a heap of verses that talk about the land leaping for joy, clapping its hands, singing and all that sort of carry on.

And what about the attitude of the people on those occasions, Mark, can you see a correlation?

Well, OK, maaaybe? Yes, OK it's true that the Bible seems to make it

clear that the land 'feels' this way when the people are happy and rejoicing too. But I have no way of substantiating that our attitude is 'felt' by the land.

But I do, Mark. I made the land. Why do you keep putting 'feel' in inverted commas like that?

Because it sounds a bit weird, not quite right somehow that the land would feel, God.

We have already established that the land is alive, Mark. Even scientists are discovering that this is true. And yes, the land does feel, and it does much more than that. You have a lot to learn about this yet.

Oh no, really?

Why oh no?

Because this is just getting weirder by the minute, God, and I have no way of justifying what I'm saying here. There are a whole bunch of white middle-aged, middle-class males (like me) who have serious issues with this kind of stuff. They won't be happy – it's way too ethnic and green. Some will even say it's new age, although no one seems to know quite what they mean by that. When Christians aren't comfortable with something, they'll often say it's 'too new age'.

Yes, they will. Rather than pass off a thing they don't understand, it would be better to ask me and get the answer straight from me, don't you think?

Yes, but most Christians aren't comfortable with that approach God, no one's taught them how.

Exactly, Mark.

God, people already think a conversation with you is pretty out there, just a bit too weird – but then you throw in this sort of stuff and those

people are likely to shut down completely.

Well, it's not weird, Mark, it's true. It's right on the nail – and anyway, it's not you who's saying it, it's me. That's the beauty of this.

It's not beautiful at all, God! People will say I'm making this up.

No, they won't. Most won't. Stop grizzling and get on with it, Mark. This is me, and others can tell that it is.

Alright fine, God.

Mark, there is plenty in the Bible to suggest that when the people are sad, bitter, jealous, angry and hateful, that the land feels that too. The Bible makes it clear that your very bones feel your attitude. And what about these verses...

"For the creation waits in eager expectation for the children of God to be revealed. For the creation was subjected to frustration, not by its own choice, but by the will of the one who subjected it, in hope that the creation itself will be liberated from its bondage to decay and brought into the freedom and glory of the children of God. We know that the whole creation has been groaning as in the pains of childbirth right up to the present time."

The land feels your attitude! Read the passage carefully, Mark, think about what it says – it talks about creation waiting, and being frustrated, in bondage to decay because of the wait. And why the wait? Because you humans are not learning what you were born to do – to be led by me. You are not having a back and forward conversation with me like Moses, the Prophets and just about every other Bible hero, and even some of the villains had. As a result, you are groaning and aching, pushing your lives up hill and the land feels that. The land groans with you.

OK. But you just said that this isn't even really about our attitude.

It's not.

What's it about then?

What did I say at the start of the conversation, Mark?

That you wanted to talk about Pākehā, Māori and the Land – and that our attitude affects the land?

Yes. And then you stopped me right there, you've spent the whole conversation interrogating me on that point so we haven't moved on.

Oops, sorry.

Don't be, I love to be interrogated and interrupted. Think about it, that's what made the prophets different – they weren't religious with me, they were human with me!

I love it when people believe I exist enough to actually engage in argument with me. It makes a welcome change from the way people use all sorts of repetition to try and attract my attention. Like I said to the Pharisees – "I'm right here in front of you". You don't need to work yourselves up to feel me. And anyway, it was a worthwhile conversation, we covered important points. But shall we continue?

'But shall we continue' – God you're not supposed to talk like that. You're supposed to be 'instructional', in command, not asking permission for anything.

Actually, Mark, I am supposed to talk like that. This sort of conversation is what you were born for. It's lucid, smart and the pinnacle of intelligence for all who engage in it. You won't do anything brainier than have a conversation with me. Nothing is brainier than this.

OK. Alright. About Māori, Pākehā and the Land God??

Yes, indeed. Your attitude toward each other, the attitude you Pākehā and Māori have toward and because of each other, is affecting your land. It always has. And it's not good.

The way you feel about each other saddens and wounds the land. You are suspicious and weary of each other. Often fed up and angry with each other. You are like spoiled children, both of you. Your demeanour (toward each other and because of each other) sours the land.

Are you looking for big repentance sessions, God?

No, Mark! That is way too easy. You all repent and feel really contrite about it all the time, but then go back to your own corners and sulk and carry on living separate lives. This is not a time for religious behaviour, no longer a time for grandstanding, it's time to get on with the job – it's time for talk.

Stop all your wailing in repentance, anger and sorrow, I've had enough of that now. It's time to talk now – about practical matters to each other and to me. About strategy, about the way forward, about how to avoid the mistakes of the past. Sitting around wailing about those mistakes was good for a season but now it's time to act.

What are we supposed to do then?

I just told you. Talk. Strategise. Plan. Acknowledge this mess, but in the way that a housewife acknowledges that a room needs tidying – she doesn't sit and wail about it. She gets on with the job, she takes stock of the problem and then gets to work so that the room is left tidy and sparkling. I want to see this land tidy and sparkling, the way it was meant to be.

When your people came, the land was largely untouched, pristine, and my plan for your coming was to help improve it – instead the result is that both of your peoples, the visitors and the hosts, are bathed in mistrust and anger, and the land feels that and sours because of it.

OK, God, at the start of this conversation when you started talking about the land and the people living on it, I had the feeling you were talking about all Kiwis, not just Māori and Pākehā, but all the other nations who continue to arrive.

Yes. Very much so. Many of you are suspicious of the new people groups arriving here. Your attitude is less than welcoming. Both of you, Pākehā and Māori, many of you feel this way toward the foreign cultures arriving here – Asian, Indian, Arabic, Muslim and so on. But I don't! I love them and am calling them here. Politicians you Christians call 'godless' and 'non-Christian' are more in tune with my plans for this nation than you are. They are sensing my Spirit calling in these new groups.

God, why do you have to challenge the commonly held perceptions all the time?

You don't need to ask that, Mark. The Bible answers that very clearly. I have always done so. Always!

OK, fair enough, but what do you want us to do about all this?

We'll come to that in other conversations, Mark. Right now I'm wanting to make you aware of the problem – and to use the problem to make you understand how many Māori feel about you Pākehā.

Oh oh.

Mark, think about the way you feel when other cultures buy up your businesses and make more money than you because they are more industrious and business-like than you are.

God, this isn't a very PC conversation.

Just be honest, Mark. Any human feels threatened when another people group moves in and begins to take power and change the culture to reflect their own.

Now, Mark, I want you to imagine how you would feel if these new people groups decided to take control of your government and industry and your land by force.

Imagine they decided to take up arms and even worse, imagine that they won. Imagine the dominant culture in New Zealand no longer being Pākehā, not even Māori, but Asian, or Indian or some other foreign culture taking control by force.

Ummm...

Think about it, Mark. Imagine if suddenly it was illegal to speak English, imagine if your children were smacked at school for speaking English. Imagine if they took your land and pushed you onto tracts of land that were no use to them. You'd lose your heart and your soul, Mark. You would be sullen and depressed and your land would reflect that.

God, I don't even know where this conversation is going? It sounds like Pākehā-bashing to me.

Mark, I do know where it's going and it's not bashing any people group. I want you to understand the effect you are all having on the land. Your poor relationships with each other are affecting the land. You need to talk and acknowledge, plan and strategise, and you need to act. You need to recognise the problems and fix them. Together. It's that simple.

So Three Guys, A Pākehā, A Māori And An Asian, All Go To See God...

And each tells him what they think is wrong with New Zealand

Mark, let's talk more about Pākehā, Māori and the land, about New Zealand.

I thought we'd finished those discussions, God??

Mark, those discussions will never be finished. Your two peoples have a lot to achieve and you haven't even really gotten started yet.

Oh. OK?

Mark, what do Pākehā think is the best solution for the relationship between Pākehā and Māori?

Well, most Pākehā Christians seem to think we should move on.

What do they mean by 'move on'?

That the grievances between our two peoples (Pākehā and Māori) are in the past now, and that we should all forgive and forget. They think Māori are nursing their hurts, not being realistic. They say Māori are in danger of 'missing the boat', in danger of missing out on what the 21st century has to offer them if they don't forget the past and move on.

Do they tell you that?

God, you know they tell me that.

Yes. They tell me that too.

Is that your point in this conversation, God?? That we all try to tell you how things should be?

Not my main point, Mark, no – far from it, but it is true, and worth noting.

OK?

Mark, what about Māori, what do they think the answer is to the situation between your two peoples?

Well, a lot of them think that Pākehā need to wake up and recognise the hurt and the grievances we've caused and…

And what, Mark?

And umm… well they think we need to recognise the injustices, stop trying to hide them and…

And what, Mark?

And maybe do something about all that, God? I think anyway. Māori are deep God and I don't want to pretend to understand exactly what they think. They think differently than us Pākehā.

Yes, they do Mark! That's an important thing to remember. So they tell you that God thinks that Pākehā need to wake up and recognise the hurt and grievances they've caused?

Yes. Well, that's the assumption anyway, that you think that it's time us Pākehā woke up.

Yes. Māori tell me that too.

So both of us, Pākehā and Māori, tell you what you should be thinking, God?

All people tell me what I should be thinking.

So that is the point of this conversation isn't it, God!! Come on admit it.

No. I already told you that, Mark. It's not the main point of this conversation.

OK then, God... what's the main point??

That neither of you, neither Pākehā nor Māori are right about this matter – you don't know my thoughts on all this. You don't know what the solution to your problem is.

OK, lovely. That'll rattle some cages, God.

Yes. There are a lot of cages in this country that need rattling, Mark. Serious rattling!

So what are we supposed to do then God? What are you really thinking about the whole Māori and Pākehā situation?

Not so fast, Mark, first I want to talk about Asian people too, and Islanders and Indians and every other people group living here, they're all important. Before I tell you what I think about Māori and Pākehā, I want to talk about all the other groups who have come to this country and the ones who are going to come in the future – because there are lots more coming, Mark. Lots and lots!

Oh no, really God?? Too many new people might change the place too much?

Yes, they'll change the place, Mark, and that's a good thing. I like it. I like new people coming. I liked it when your people arrived, and I like it just as much when these new people arrive. This isn't your country, it's mine. You're a guest here, all of you are. I love having you, I want you to make yourselves at home, but I want you to treat my other guests with the same respect I treat you. And if I want to invite even more guests (and I do) then I want them to make themselves just as much at home as you have. It's not your place, it's mine. You're all welcome guests.

OK, God.

Mark, the whole state of affairs in New Zealand looks like a mess to you doesn't it?

Yes, a bit.

Why Mark?

Because the old harmony between Māori and Pākehā, the harmony I remember as a kid seems to have gone and now our relationship is a mess and it's getting complicated because there are heaps and heaps of other people groups arriving. So there's not much harmony and I don't know... there doesn't seem to be a clear identity of what us Kiwis look like anymore.

Mark, there never was harmony between Māori and Pākehā when you were a kid. Harmony is a two-part thing – two parts working together, each part making the other stronger, and that has never really been the case with Pākehā and Māori.

Oh...

Just because things suited you Pākehā when you were a kid, it doesn't mean it suited Māori. Māori simply tolerated you Pākehā; pretended they were happy and put up with their lot because you didn't offer them any choice. But now a new generation has stood up and is demanding answers. That's making it uncomfortable for everyone, particularly you Pākehā.

So God, you do agree with Māori that us Pākehā need to wake up??

No, I don't.

So are us Pākehā right then??

No. You're not right either. Before I talk about who's right, I want to talk about the other people – Asians, Indians, Islanders and everyone else...

So are they the ones who are right??

No, they're not right either. What do they, those new groups, tell you that I think about the situation in New Zealand?

God, I think they say that us Pākehā and Māori need to sort out our problems because it causes disharmony in New Zealand. It concerns them, it makes their lives less enjoyable, they wonder why us Pākehā and Māori are so unhappy together. They think that we need to sort things out.

Yes. They tell me that too.

Are they right, God??

No, they're wrong too. All of you, Pākehā, Māori and all the other peoples – Asian, Islander, Indian, Arabic, you're all wrong about what I think about the situation in New Zealand. All wrong. I do not think what any of you think.

Well, what do you think then God??

You really want to know what I think?

Yes, God! Come on!

Do you want to know why you're all wrong?? Each people group's common perceptions are wrong – do you want to know what's wrong with all of your perceptions, Mark?

Yes. I think so anyway.

It's pretty blimmen simple, Mark.

GOD!!! You do not say 'blimmen'.

Mark, this is you interpreting my voice. You heard what I said and your word for what I said is blimmen. In these conversations you are the interpreter. Interpreters use their own language to express what the speaker is saying. Another interpreter might have used a different word.

Yes, but God, you wouldn't let me say blimmen!!

Really Mark? I let you do everything else you do :)

Mark, the thing that's wrong between all of your people in New Zealand, is very simple. Any counsellor could tell you. It's a common problem in any relationship. What you Pākehā and Māori and all you other people groups need to do is very simple, and not nearly as complex as you make it. It's just relationship 101.

Does that mean we don't need to ask you, God?

No! It means you do need to ask me. After all this time, you still haven't figured it out, and if Pākehā, Māori and all the other people groups in New Zealand don't start asking me about this and listening to my answers, then you will never figure this out. Never!

OK, tell us then, God! What do we need to do??

Mark, the first thing you all need to do, is look at is what's wrong with your current thinking.

What is wrong with it, God?

That's easy to spot, Mark, because you all think the same thing.

No we don't, God!! That's the problem, we all think totally different things.

No, you don't, not really. You all think that it's the others who need to do something to sort this mess out. Pākehā think that Māori need to forget the past and face the future. You're wrong!

Māori think you Pākehā need to wake up and realise the horrible things you've done (and you have done plenty, Mark) but they're wrong too. And all the other people groups think they can see the problem – they wish you, Pākehā and Māori, would sort out your differences to bring harmony to New Zealand, but they're wrong too.

The problem with all of your thinking, is that you're convinced the others need to sort themselves out. And you're wrong. The others can't sort anything out on their own, and neither can you. You all have to get together and sort this problem out, *together*. You all need to take action together instead of waiting for the other to do something, or trying to do something on your own. You need to take action together. Māori, Pākehā, Asian, Islander, Indian, Arabic and every other culture in the country. You all need to take action, together!

There have been all sorts of horrors committed and hurts suffered. But the real problem is that you think the other person needs to do something. But they can't! None of you can fix this without the others. I put you all together here for an amazing purpose, but before we get to that, I'd like you to sort this mess out, together. Stop waiting for the other to sort out their problems. Help them.

You need to do this together. You can't do it any other way.

OK, wow.

It is time to move forward, Mark, way past time – you Pākehā are right about that much. But Pākehā also need to accept that the past is littered with horrific injustice engineered, carried out and then comfortably overlooked by everyday Pākehā – Māori are right about that much. The two of your peoples need to sort out your differences (together) so others can live here more happily and productively – Asians, Islanders, Indians and all the other groups are right about that.

But you're all wrong waiting for the others to sort out the problem – they can't and they won't. Not without your help. You're all in this together. All three of you need help from all of the others. You need to sort this out together. You need to move forward and make New Zealand what it is meant to be on the world stage. I brought all of your people groups here to make this nation an example of how to meld different people groups into a great, harmonious, wealthy, powerful nation that welcomes in many. 'God defend our free land'. Make it so, Mark. Sort out your problems together and make it free.

Want To Have Your Own Back And Forth Conversation With God About Māori, Pākehā And The Land?

See back section of this book: Page 181

Includes: Six amazing interviews with God about how to have your own conversation with him. Hear what God has to say to you about all this.

Innocent blood cries out from your land, New Zealand

When will you address this?

God, every time I drive past that sign that says 'Te Porere Redoubt', I feel like you're saying I should go in and have a look.

Yes.

But I've never really got time, God.

No.

OK, so the other day I finally drove in to the Te Porere Redoubt for a look.

Yes finally, Mark.

And as I drove down the little track, I think I heard you say there had been a great travesty of justice at that place...?

Yes. I said justice had not been served at Te Porere.

OK God, so when I got out of my truck I discovered two things that surprised me: Te Porere was a Māori Redoubt, not a Pākehā (white European) one, and it was there that the famous Māori warrior chief Te Kooti staged his last stand against us Pākehā. I've driven past that place countless times and yet I had no idea.

Mark, I haven't forgotten about Te Porere, but first I want you to explain to readers how to pronounce his name.

Really, God?? A lot of my readers think that Te Kooti was just a mischievous 'native rebel'.

A name is important, Mark. To pronounce a name correctly shows respect, and actually Te Kooti himself deserves respect.

Alright, well the dictionary says his name should be pronounced 'Te Kortee', but us Pākehā sound it like 'Te Kootee'. When Māori pronounce his name they say it with respect, and they seem to add a second 'OR' sound, sort of like 'Te Kor-or-ti'.

Yes. Both those Māori options are acceptable, but the way you Pākehā pronounce it is not.

This is not a good start, God! I was hoping to keep this conversation sounding balanced and diplomatic. I sensed you wanted it to appeal to both sides.

I do, and it will, Mark. It will appeal to you Pākehā because I will use logic you can't deny. And it will appeal to Māori because I will identify issues they think I have forgotten. But neither of you will be comfortable by the time we've finished, this is one of those discussions.

Well, God, that night after I'd been to Te Porere, I did a heap of reading to find out what really happened there, and honestly, I couldn't find any evidence of gross injustice.

And yet you heard me right, Mark, justice was not served! It seldom ever is in war.

Did you say never?

No. But seldom. Justice was not served at Te Porere. Men died needlessly. One man was retaliating against injustice. But as is the case with most humans, his retaliation was far from just.

God, I wish you hadn't said that, Māori hold Te Kooti up to be a great man.

He was, many men are great, Mark. But none are perfect. Te Kooti was far from perfect, he was like many military generals, he fought against injustice, and yet his actions too, were often unjust. Both sides took lives that should not have been taken. That's the way of war, justice is seldom served.

Most wars start with an act of injustice against an innocent people. Then someone responds violently to stop the injustice. Their response is understandable, yet often equally wrong. Te Kooti was treated unjustly, his rights were violated by men who should not have been given the authority to do that to him. That's where the injustice started, but not where it stopped.

His retaliation against their treatment was equally unfair, the blood of innocent women and children was spilled at Poverty Bay. You Pākehā called it a massacre, and it was; and yet five years earlier, when your own 'gallant' troops mowed down innocent women and children at Rangiaowhia and then again at Orakau, you preferred to call those occasions 'battles'. The word massacre is strangely absent when Pākehā talk about those times. A bit of advice to Pākehā and Māori; If you lie to yourselves about your history, you cease to know who you really are.

God, you didn't have to be quite so blatant. Pākehā will think I'm stirring up trouble, the vast majority of us have no idea about Rangiaowhia or Orakau, no one ever admitted the truth about those stories when we were at school.

Yes, some people, Pākehā and Māori, will think you're stirring up trouble, but there are plenty more who already know it's time you both took responsibility. This country is drenched in blood. Pākehā vs Māori, and before that Māori vs Māori. Way too much blood spilled by way too many of you! Both of you are far from innocent. Both responsible for rape, murder, massacre and theft. It has to stop. But it won't unless you work together to stop it. Simple as that. Both sides are at fault, and have been at fault since the start of this mess.

You are both like angry children, both as bad as each other. When I try to speak to you about this, both Pākehā and Māori shout in your hearts, "he started it!!" When humans fight, it doesn't matter who started it, pretty quickly both sides are at fault. Although one starts it, the other soon re-starts it, and so on.

God, really? All these Pākehā/Māori conversations have always been very diplomatic, but now you seem stern and cross??

I'm not stern and I'm not cross, but I'm definitely insistent. It's time, time to cut to the chase. Te Kooti was wronged, and so in retaliation he wronged the Pākehā back. And then the Pākehā wronged him back, and so on. Every response shed more innocent blood. The land aches and groans, it cries out under the weight of the blood that each of you has spilled. Neither of you won at any of your battles, not at Te Porere, nor Rangiriri, nor Orakau, nor Gate Pa – every time you fought each other, you both lost.

When each battle was over, the Māori went home to tend their crops. They weren't savages, they were farmers with more extensive and profitable land holdings than you Pākehā. The moment they'd gone, your generals would declare a victory, whether or not you had won. Many of your 'victories' had nothing to do with the rules of war, they were in fact a sham.

But even your great generals quickly became disillusioned. They soon realised the politicians had planned the war to justify taking Māori land. They needed it to satisfy the demands of the white settlers. No one is without guilt in this sorry mess, Mark. It's a fact, check your history, General Cameron soon realised what Governor Grey and his cohorts were really up to. You all need to be aware, both sides, you need to accept the reality of what happened in New Zealand, and then start fixing the mess. Together. Teach each other the truth about your history, truth always sets you free.

Māori were, and still are, better fighters than you, but there were so many more of you, that after the battle was over, the battle which they often won, you still came and occupied their land and took their goods.

Hang on. God, this is very pro-Māori, you're putting all the blame on us Pākehā!

I am pro Māori, Mark. and I'm pro Pākehā too, I'm pro-Human. But you're not, neither of you. Pākehā and Māori are both so wrapped up in your own agendas that you have become virtually blind to the other.

Justice was not served at Te Porere, it was just like every other battle you fought against each other. Lives were lost and blood shed for no reason. What is required, Mark, is simple: Discussion. Working together. Being prepared to admit you're wrong (both of you), because you're both very wrong. If Pākehā and Māori look back on your respective histories, you will stumble over things that horrify you. If you look back with honesty, then you can look forward in a way that heals, together.

Māori have covered their own historical guilt against this land by pointing out the horror of what you Pākehā did. And you Pākehā have used your religion and your churches to whitewash your own actions.

You've pretended a unity that has never been there and a love that is only surface deep. In your churches you've tricked the Māori to accept their lot, you've pretended love and urged them it's time to move on, to forgive and forget.

Yes, it's time to move on, but with honesty. You both need to stop pretending the other is the one at fault. You're both at fault. You need to start owning the harms you have done in this place.

God, are you talking about the Māori history of massacre before us Pākehā arrived?

Mark, I have much to discuss with Māori, and because they're human, a lot of it isn't pretty, but that's between them and I, and nothing to do with you right now. You just focus on your own mess.

You Pākehā were never the clear winner in battle, you passed laws that allowed you to steal their land, yet call it confiscation. Then your churches proclaimed my blessing over the land you had stolen from the children of those you killed. That's history, any scholar can point that out for you. The politicians and military heroes you celebrate from that era, are in reality condemned by the bloodshed they inflicted on this land.

But God, what about all the injustice Māori have committed over the years too – the crime, the gangs – I suppose you're going to say that's our fault too??

No. That's their fault. Although much of it is an angry response to your greed and political injustice, you're right. Those things are just as unacceptable as your massacres and land theft. You're both wrong, Mark, and you're both right. There needs to be a balance of power and an agreement of purpose.

After all the injustices you have committed against each other, the position of control was assumed and held tight by you Pākehā. You pretended to treaty, but had no such end in mind, you were unwilling to stop until you had all the land and power. For all of their faults, Māori could see that the agreement you had asked for at Waitangi was a ruse, it meant nothing to you.

And yet, God, I think you're saying that we should not be grovelling to each other?

No more grovelling, Mark. Now it's time for action. We have business to do, Māori, Pākehā and God working together. We need to get on with it. Each of you needs to acknowledge the horror you have inflicted on others in this land - and then help each other fix the mess. Then finally, you'll be able to get on with the purpose I brought both your peoples here for.

You cannot build a relationship around saying sorry! Sorry isn't a relationship, it's just a tool. If you pretend there is no mess, then you can't fix it. If you pretend it's the other's fault, then you can't fix it either. But if you both recognise that this mess belongs to you, then you can help each other to clean it up. The cleanup is just the beginning.

I brought you here, both of you, because I could see that you would be better together, Māori and Pākehā. So no more grovelling, the time for sorry is over. Now it's time to acknowledge the extent of the mess and clean it up together before it damages more of your children.

Special Bonus Book

Want to hear God's voice more clearly?

The following pages are our special bonus Book, *'What they never told you about how to have a back and forth conversation with God like a friend'.* Others wanting to hear God's voice more clearly, have found these pages a huge help. They include answers to all the FAQs about how to have a conversation with God.

What They Never Told you

How having a conversation with God healed our Marriage...... 185

The conversation with God that healed our Marriage 191

Six interviews with God about how to do this

1. Yes you can hear God talk to you 199
2. You don't have to be perfect to hear him 207
3. How do you know it's real? 213
4. What sort of question's can you ask him?..................... 221
5. Is it always clear what God is saying? 227
6. What to do when you think God has broken a promise to you.. 235

How to have your own conversation with God

How to have a back and forth conversation with God........... 245

How to deal with Doubt.. 249

Does a conversation with God have to be in writing? 253

What can I have a conversation with God about? 255

Why isn't this common?... 258

What to do if God doesn't seem to answer....................... 259

What to do if God's answers sound too good? 261

How often can I have a conversation with God? 263

Why is there so much doubt and opposition?.................... 265

What if I hear God wrong? 267

Why don't I have to be a better person first?.................. 269

Why does God sound differently to each of us?................. 270

Is it difficult?.. 271

Important life lessons from the conversations

Life is a smorgasbord.. 274

The better you choose to feel, the better you will feel............ 275

If you pass kindness onto others, they will too 276
A messy room is hardly life threatening 277
Driving a Kenworth and a conversation with God 278
Annette's Story 280
Maggie's Story 281
Ollie's Story 282
Peacekeepers stay quiet 283
Offence is more often taken 285
The Bible and conversations with God
A few things we have learned about the conversations 287
What does the Bible say about listening to God? 291
Bible Heroes and Villains 295
The Freedom Diaries 299
The Freedom Assignment 301
Mark and Miriam Speak to your Church or Group 303

How Having A Conversation With God Healed Our Marriage After Five Years Apart

The real story behind The Freedom Diaries

MARK'S STORY: In 2010 my life went down the plughole in a single day. After 27 years and five great kids, my wife left me. I screamed out in terror to God and to my amazement he spoke back, so clearly I could understand what he said. He said so much I had to write it down to keep up. He was warm and kind yet made it clear I had caused the problem. And most incredible he promised she'd be back.

I argued. I told him expecting her back was a pipe dream. I told him it couldn't be all my fault because there are two sides to every story. He agreed there are two sides, but he'd only be discussing my side with me and then he assured me again that Miriam would come back. At first I was comforted by his words, but weeks went by, and then eventually years, and still no sign of Miriam. I argued daily with God and told him that the voice I was hearing was obviously not his. But he kept gently reassuring me that she'd be back.

Eventually I realised I was either going mad or this really was a conversation with God, but how could it be God if my wife still wasn't back?

I worried I was deceived so I showed my conversations with God to senior Christians. They were convinced I was hearing God and those who tried it themselves were amazed to discover that suddenly they too were having their own back and forward conversations with God.

Many of them urged me to put my conversations in a book, so I did and *The Freedom Diaries* was born. It became a best seller and readers said it changed their lives. Yet after four long years Miriam still hadn't come back. That cunning spirit Doubt continually taunted me, he said I'd obviously heard God wrong, he mocked me that Miriam hadn't come back and said the book was a farce.

MIRIAM'S STORY: And then just like God said I would, I came back, five whole years after I left. But I have to say, that for the first few years after I left Mark I was floating two feet off the ground. I was free!

I know that sounds terrible, but our marriage was typical of many. After 27 years together and five children I was at the point in my life - our life actually - that I could no longer stay with Mark. Lots of little things built up over the years until finally I couldn't cope anymore and I felt my only option was to leave.

In the first four and half years we were apart I never had any intention or inclination to go back. I was happy!! I no longer had to think of the 'right' answers. I had my own personal growth with God and an awesome relationship with Him. I was brought up by parents who loved God and leaving your husband was not the done thing so it was a very big decision for me. Although at the time there seemed no other option, I realise looking back that I had two other options; I could have stayed but that would have seen us in the same mess today. We would be no further ahead, maybe even worse off. There would have been no stumbling across the conversation with God, no Freedom Diaries and no spreading the news about the conversation to others.

The other option would have been to have a conversation with God but of course, like most Christians, neither of us knew that it was possible. If we had we could have let him explain in words we could understand how to sort the whole big mess out without having to separate.

But often it's not until you are absolutely desperate and can see no solution, that you will find God in the midst of it all, or more importantly that he will find you.

There was one other thing that would have helped me, a thing I learned once we were apart, but would have helped me if I'd understood it back then. That would have been to look for good. I could have looked for the things that I had first loved about Mark. If I had focused on those good things about him, one good thing would have added to another until a new picture of Mark began to develop and the big bad picture of our marriage would have begun to recede.

I have learned during this time that if we look for good in any circumstance it is always there waiting to be found. The more you focus on and look for good in people or situations the better you will feel and function and the clearer your head will be. Looking for good and practising kindness helps us, it helps our marriage. If I had understood the incredible power of that back then, things might have been different.

While we were apart I discovered the power of looking for the good, it changed my life and made it great! It was living this way that lead me to realise that I too was having a back and forward conversation with God. As I began to see the good in myself I realised that God would actually want to talk to me. As a result I am now ever enthusiastic to encourage and build people up. To tell them "you ARE worth it and you DO have choices and God is right there waiting to talk TO you ABOUT you."

Until we separated, I had been involved in the family business and being a mum. Suddenly I was on my own and I needed a job badly. Before the children I had been a nurse and then a police constable. To go back to either of these professions I would need to retrain but I needed something right now. Friends in the kiwifruit industry asked if I would help out in the bin dump during picking season. I loved the outdoors and I loved the job.

One particular day I drove into an orchard that had a bin dump at the very back of the orchard - it was a very narrow, winding, muddy road. When I got in to the site there was a huge truck and trailer parked there - an 18 speed tractor unit with a b-train combination on the back with its curtains all open and half loaded with kiwi fruit bins. I was blown away! "How did you get in here??" "Not by helicopter lady, same way as you did!" I was hooked. I decided right there on the spot that I was going to drive one of these beauties and over the course of the next year I got my truck and trailer licence and now drive big rigs for a hobby (well, it's my job actually because I get paid to do it!)

At the beginning of 2014, after Mark and I had been apart for four years, our youngest daughter Freedom was going to attend Mt Aspiring College in Wanaka. She was the only one still at home so I went too! Not to school but I got a great job down there driving a beautiful Kenworth.

Moving to Wanaka in the South Island of New Zealand meant I would be 1500kms from Mark. It was a fantastic move for me. I no longer had to hear his big motorbike roaring up the road or have him knocking at the door to mow my lawns. From the time we moved down in January until Easter that year I barely gave Mark a thought. I was happy and loving my life.

Then at Easter time he rode down with some biking buddies to the 'Warbirds over Wanaka' air show. He txted me to see if he could bring his mates round for a coffee. It was nice to meet them and then off they all went back to the North Island. After they left, I became very unsettled and bothered. My mum was staying with me and she asked what the problem was. I told her I had a horrible feeling I might have to go back to Mark. This is terrible but I felt like washing my mouth out!! Mum told me I would need to sort this out with God – that he wouldn't 'make' me do anything I didn't want to do. She said that I would know the right thing to do and have a peace about it.

Then three weeks later Mark emailed me a conversation he and God had about us. After I read that email, I had no doubt in my mind what my next step was. It wasn't just me or Mark feeling this, but actually God himself was talking us back together. And when he talks somehow peace comes. That was May. Mark and

I had conversations with God and he told us both to put our marriage back together slowly, to remember our adult kids would be watching and to do things in a way that would be acceptable to them. So we shared the whole thing with them and in December that year I went back to Mark with our kid's blessing – just as God (unbeknown to me) had promised Mark I would.

FOOTNOTE: God says that many many people gain hope from hearing us read the conversation with God that put our marriage back together, and that to include it here will give even more people hope if they read it too. Please note that one of the very important things God stresses to Mark is the importance of talk–talk with God – backwards and forwards – and talk with each other backwards and forwards. God promised it would heal our marriage and day by day it really is. We both hope that the same back and forward talk with God and with each other will heal your situation too.

The Conversation With God That Healed Our Marriage

I tried to persuade God that I shouldn't send this conversation to Miriam but he insisted. Three days later she replied saying she knew it was God and that day we began to put our marriage back together

God, I've been dreading this conversation all afternoon since lunch time when you told me you wanted me to have it.

Why?

Because this is about Miriam and I. This is much more important than all the conversations in the book all put together. They're nothing compared to this one.

It's what I want to discuss.

But God, you're wanting me to send this to Miriam. This is stuff that you and I've been talking about for four and a half years, but you never let me tell Miriam. And now suddenly, when I'm least expecting it, you tell me to pass this on. I don't get it.

It's what I want. The time's right for reasons you don't know about. Just carry on.

OK. Well, all these years I'm sure you've told me to wait for Miriam, but you've never let me tell Miriam that you told me to wait - and keep telling me to wait when it hurts too much to wait. So why tell her now after all these years?

It's time.

OK, and I'm convinced you've told me to expect... can I really say

this here?

Yes.

You really want me to send this to Miriam?

Really.

So do you want me to say what I've always felt you've been saying about us? I ask you about us every day, many, many times a day – I have done so for the whole horrible four years. And now you want me to say what I've heard you say??

Yes.

OK, I'm pretty sure, well actually I'm very sure you've said to expect her back. That it's only a matter of time, and if I was prepared to wait it would happen. Every single day I ask you, often many times in a day, and you always say wait, she comes back. When I ask what about free will you say that it's nothing to do with you making Miriam do anything, that she's free to do whatever she wants, but that you also know the future. Have I said too much?

No, that's fine.

OK. So God I saw Miriam at the weekend and I realised that for the first time I don't even know if I want her back. The hurt has gone on for so long, and been so deep.

So Mark now, finally, you know how Miriam felt.

Truly? I honestly hurt her this bad? Made her feel this rejected? I had no idea God.

It was as bad as it's been for you. Actually worse.

Oh man. I hate me. I'm speechless. I didn't know I was capable of that. I'm so sorry. I don't know what to do then God. I can't even imagine

how that must have felt for Miriam.

It devastated her, crippled her.

So are you saying it's too late, too much damage done? Do you want us to go our separate ways then??

No.

I don't get it. What do you want??

I want you to reconcile.

How? After so much hurt?

Talk. You have both hurt each other so badly now. But if you want to rebuild, I do too. And talk is all it will take. Talk with me, and talk with each other.

God, this is making me cry, but I think it will just make Miriam angry with me.

Mark, down under all that hurt and anger she still loves you.

Really God? I don't think so. I think I'm making that bit up.

No you're not. Mark, you leave what Miriam feels to me and her. I want her to talk to me about her feelings. We'll sort through that. But I'm telling you that the two of you need to talk. I want you to talk. If you're prepared to talk, you can rebuild. Slowly and carefully you can do it. It's up to the two of you. But if you want to, you can. Do you want to do it?

You know I do. But Miriam doesn't think I really love her.

Of course not. And you didn't think she loved you either.

No. I thought she despised me. I felt that way for years. I felt that she thought I was just a joke.

But what have I shown you in the last four years?

That she loved me. That nobody has ever loved me as much as Miriam did. That she tried and tried, but that I didn't believe her love.

But did you love her?

Yes! You know I did. With all my heart, that's why it hurt so much to think she didn't love me.

And Mark, the very same pain was cutting Miriam to bits at the same time. Both of you loved each other. So much. So very very much. And yet both of you, at the same time, doubted the other's love. How do you think that happened?

I'm pretty sure you've told me that the same demon told us both the same lie – he whispered that the person we loved most didn't love us back. That he wanted our marriage destroyed and our family cut in pieces, and he knew that if he patiently told that lie to us. Day in, day out, year in year out, that eventually one or both of us would break. I almost broke first, and I guess that pushed Miriam over the brink?

Mark, you both messed your marriage up.

But you've told me that it was my fault.

It was. I'm only prepared to talk to you about your fault. I'll talk to Miriam, not you, about her fault. Do you understand? You both got yourselves into this mess by believing that the other didn't love you. You both believed a lie. A simple hateful lie that destroys families. He gave you a double dose of his voice because he could see that the two of you are destined to learn and then teach others how to hear my voice.

He needed to focus on and destroy your marriage, before your marriage destroyed so much of what he has carefully built over hundreds of years. The two of you together are destined to teach others to hear my voice. He has spent hundreds of years teaching people that my voice cannot be easily heard. So now, if you want me to, I am going to use the two of you to destroy so much of the destruction he has planned for humanity, just with the simple act of teaching others to hear my voice. And if you'll work with me in that way, then you will also dismantle a huge part of his specific plans to hurt your kids and their kids. Do you want that?

I do. But if I've hurt Miriam worse than this, then she probably won't.

You leave Miriam and I to decide what she wants. We'll decide that together. But I can get you both out of this mess if you'll both let me. Talk. That's what I want. If you're both prepared to do that, you can reconcile, rebuild and restore your family and your marriage. It will be more powerful, more amazing, and have more effect on others than it has ever done before. But only if that's what you both want. It's entirely up to you. The two of you. There's no condemnation if you don't want this. But it's what I want. And if you want to know how, I'll show you. Nothing is impossible with me.

Can you see the miracle, Mark? This situation with which he hoped to destroy you and your kids, instead...? Instead I have used the situation to teach you both to hear me so much more clearly than ever before. And now, armed with that new ability, if you let me, I can use the two of you to destroy him with so much more power than you had before. The two of you together, unstoppable because now you can hear my voice! Not just you, but Miriam too. She hears equally well. Yet differently. You need each other's ability to hear me to complete the picture.

But Mark, you'll need to talk. With each other, and with me. Lots and lots and lots of talk.

But God, she doesn't like talk.

Yes she does. If she's allowed she does. You'll need to listen to Miriam. A lot. You'll need to let her talk. And she'll need to be understanding of your fear of silence, and to gently remind you to be quiet and listen to her. She will need to be strong about that. And you'll need to listen. But you both need to talk. A lot. And as you do, you need to talk to me and to report to each other what I'm saying to you.

Can you see that, Mark? The only way to put this back together is to have many many many conversations with me – individually and then eventually together.

Don't hurry. Do this slowly. Putting the two conversations, mine with you, and mine with Miriam together will show you both the way forward. That's the only way it will work. Lots of talk. To me, individually to me, and then together. You didn't talk with each other much before, but if you're prepared to do so, you will heal this situation. You will remake hope for everyone around you. You will both be stunned at how many lives will be changed forever if you're prepared to take this step. Together.

Apart I will bless you and give you whatever you want. But together you will bless me and give me what I want.

OK. God do you want me to send this to Miriam tonight?

No.

God?

No.

Tomorrow?

Yes.

Six Interviews With God About How To Do This

How to have a back and forth conversation with God

(The simple steps that no one ever told us)

1
Yes, You Can Hear God Talk To You In Whole Sentences About Whatever You Ask

How to have a back a forth conversation with God without having to be sinless first.

Mark, I want to ask you some questions. Your answers will help people understand how to have a conversation with me. You know that anyone is easily able to hear me speak in their minds – so clearly that they'll understand exactly what I'm saying. I want you to give them pointers so they can try this themselves.

OK.

So first explain how you started doing this.

OK, I had already been writing down all the things I thought you were saying but not in actual conversation. Then I went to a camp where they asked me to read a Bible verse and then write a list of questions to you about the verse. That all seemed OK. But then they asked me to write down your answers!

How did you feel about that?

I thought they were mad. It seemed like conjuring up your voice rather than waiting for it. But I decided to give it a go because a friend I respected had urged me to go to this camp. But I didn't think it would work.

Then what happened?

Well, I got out my pen, and in disbelief that I was silly enough to try something like this, I began to write.

And?

Your answers came thick and fast. I could hardly believe it. Here I was writing your words. And I could tell it was you.

But you wanted to believe it wasn't me. So how could you be so sure?

For that very reason. I wanted to prove the idea stupid, so when I could feel that the words I was writing were coming from you, I was blown away.

Did I move the pen?

No nothing like that. I've got control of the pen.

So how did it actually work?

I'd write a question to you. I think the first one was something like 'God, are you saying in this verse in Philippians 3 that my Christianity is not enough, that I need to push further? That in this verse, Paul was saying, like Bono sings, that he still hadn't found what he was looking for?'

And then what happened?

I wrote your answer. And I could tell as I wrote that I was hearing you and writing your words. The act of writing seemed to be an act of faith. It seemed totally crazy and yet I knew it was you. I'd start writing your answer by writing some words to get my mind moving and receptive to what you were saying. Maybe my name, or the obvious beginning of a sentence. Something like 'What I am saying, Mark, is...'

OK? Then what?

I'd just keep writing and you'd provide the words. Your first answer I wrote came something like this; *'What I am saying, Mark, is yes,* *your heart cries out for more because there is more. You're just touching the surface. You're right to be frustrated with normal Christianity. I want you frustrated.'* **I started writing to prove this wouldn't work, but as I wrote I discovered it did. It was so obvious that it was you. I wanted to doubt, but I couldn't.**

Something happened in your mind and heart when you saw that this was true?

Yes, something exploded in my mind. I thought if I can hear this clearly from God about a Bible verse, I wonder if he'll answer any question this clearly? I had heaps of questions about my life, my family and business, and the thought that I could get them answered this clearly was incredible.

So what did you do?

I asked you a whole bunch of questions, about stuff I was worried about.

And what happened?

Two things. You answered. Oh man did you answer. It was fantastic!! But the other thing that happened wasn't so fantastic. I asked the people who ran the camp if I was getting it right. Do these sound like the answers of God? They said I must leave those sorts of questions about my personal life in God's hands. They told me to seek first the kingdom of God, the inference being that stuff about my personal life isn't the kingdom of God.

And?

Well, I thought something seemed a bit wrong. We can't box you like that. I wondered if Religion had stepped in without those people realizing. Religion suggests that when things are dear to us, family, health etc, that you're not pleased, and to get your approval we need to focus on 'spiritual' things.

So what did you do?

Well; you'd already answered a whole bunch of personal questions so I decided not to argue, but just to keep asking you questions about everything anyway. I was so excited. A conversation with God. What could be better!

You wanted to talk about stuff that was important to me! Not boring 'holy stuff'. The more you spoke, the more I realised that you do *s*peak about everything we want to know.

So the people at the camp were right about their basic 'writing it down' approach?

Absolutely. So right! They had discovered this idea that God will converse with us whatever we're like. They opened up to me the most incredible thing that has ever happened to me. That you want to converse all the time, all day long, about every little thing, right down to whether to buy the expensive salt or the cheaper one at the supermarket.

OK. So what was the next development?

I started writing questions to you, about everything. All day long. So much in my life was going terribly wrong. You'd made me some amazing promises about family and business, but none of them seemed to be coming true.

And what was the outcome?

I started getting answers about everything.

How did you know it was me?

I could just tell. You sort of can. A friend of mine who has started to converse with you too describes it as a feeling of 'satisfaction'. You just know when it's God. The odd time when it wasn't, I could quickly sense that.

Explain?

It might seem you'd said something really encouraging. It might sound like you were confirming a promise you'd made some other time. So I'd enthusiastically write it down, but the moment the words hit the page it wouldn't seem right.

That really confused me.

So?

I'd ask you again. And it might still seem you were saying that, but it would still seem wrong. So I'd ask again. And eventually, as I wrote the words, I would know this time whether or not it was you. Yes or no, I'd know.

What did you learn from that?

That the enemy will try to sound like you to put me off track.

Why would he want to do that?

Subterfuge. This is war. He tried the same thing on you, he quoted verses to you. If he can use a truth to get me listening to his voice, and make me think his voice is yours, then he can begin to take me down the wrong track.

So sometimes you'd end up asking me the same question again and again before you broke through and heard the right answer? And you always seemed to know when you needed to do that?

Yes. I'd be terribly frustrated thinking 'how can anyone possibly hear from God with this confusion?' And yet if I kept at it, I'd always end up knowing what you'd said.

People who don't like this idea of a conversation with you say that if there's confusion, it can't be from God. That threw me at first but then I realised they were just as confused as anyone else. And

I remembered the angel who came to Daniel. He'd had to battle a demon for three weeks before Daniel could hear your answer. I realised that hearing you speak into my mind is going to be a battle. But what a fantastic thing to battle for!

Then you moved to speaking my answers out loud too. How did it happen?

I was writing questions to you and then writing your answers. It was happening all day long and I realised it was getting impractical to do it all the time. I like the writing because it helps me think out exactly what you're saying, but when I'm riding my motorbike, it means stopping to write. I might be flying down the road on my motorbike, having a full blown conversation with you. It was silly. I was riding and stopping all the time. Crazy!

I asked you and you seemed to say it would be OK – instead of writing, to speak my questions to you and then speak your answers back. I could see this was a sort of self-prophecy. Something my friend David Garratt confirmed a couple of years later. You'd been talking to him too about what he called 'self-prophecy'.

This sounds so silly and religious now, but I would speak out my question to you, and then lay a hand on my own head and prophesy back your answer.

But it worked?

Well yes. I could tell it was you. I was a bit nervous about it at first, but I could tell it was you because it felt exactly the same as when I ever speak some sort of prophecy to someone else. It was the same God talking. It was you. But this time it was a prophecy to myself. Kind of weird. But obviously true.

But then you got less religious?

Yes, eventually I could hear you say relax. You said to forget the hand thing, just speak what I tell you.

And do you have to double check my answers when you speak them out loud?

Often. Often I'm not sure if I've heard you or not, so I come back repeatedly until the answer is clear. When it's clear I can suddenly sense that in my spirit.

I told you something which has really helped. What was that?

That this is a conversation between the infinite God (you), and a finite human (me). And you want me to be me and you to be you in that conversation. So I have to be relaxed about the fact that I'm human. Relaxed that the things I want to ask you are human things and not churchy, missionary, religious, 'Godish' sorts of things. Relaxed that I want to ask you about my wife, my kids, my business, my supermarket shopping etc. You told me to leave you to be God, and enjoy that I'm human because that's the way you love me to be. If you didn't, you'd have created me as something else.

> *'So God created man in his own image, in the image of God he created him; male and female he created them//God saw all that he had made, and it was very good.'* GENESIS 1:27 AND 31

2
You Don't Have To Be Perfect To Hear Him

Mark, I want to keep interviewing you about this, so that others can have practical tips on listening to me. What have you noticed to be the differences in your life as a result of listening?

Well, the good side is there is such an overpowering awareness of you being near. Right there. Every day I experience you making yourself evident to a level I had experienced only a handful of times in my whole life before that.

I mean obviously you were here all the time before this, but now when I listen, you make yourself known. And right now I find myself in a situation of my own doing, where I need to hear exactly what you're saying to get through.

I've been waiting all my life for you to make yourself more evident, and blaming my sinfulness as the reason you didn't. But now you tell me that wasn't the issue. You were waiting for me to listen so you could make yourself evident.

It's fantastic. I can ask you questions about anything that's happening in my life, and you answer! Sometimes you even tell me what's going to happen next.

What's that like? Does it make everything OK?

It does and it doesn't. It makes more sense of what's happening. You show me why things are taking place in my life, you show me when to let things pass and when to take some sort of action.

But sometimes it doesn't make everything OK?

Well no. You don't just fix everything. I had this idea that the closer we got the better everything would be. But it's not like that. If something's not right you don't just fix it. You show me how I've made it wrong, and then you encourage me to fix it myself.

How?

Well, you often point out what I've done to hurt others. I used to always come and complain to you about them, but you don't seem interested. You want to show me how I've hurt them and what I can do to mend the hurt and build bridges. And how to work on changing so I hurt them less and less.

But is listening to me worth it?

Yes.

Why?

Because what else is there? What could possibly match a conversation with the Creator? Imagine you met an angel. And you knew it was an angel. And the angel said to you, 'God's waiting around the corner to talk to you. I'll take you to him.' It'd be like you'd won the lottery.

Now that happens to me every day. All day. God's waiting around the corner to talk to me. Actually you're waiting in my room, in my car, on the motorbike, in my office. Always there.

Even though life doesn't suddenly get all better, I know I'm getting closer to what I'm on the planet for. Listening to you. The relationship that comes from a conversation with you is what I was put here for. I'm finally hearing more and more of what *you* have to say. It's not always nice or comfortable, but it's awesome too.

What sort of questions am I comfortable with you asking?

I used to always be at you to 'fix this, sort this out, make that person do this'.

But when I realised I could actually hear you speak whenever I wanted to, I started asking 'are you going to fix this?' 'What are you going to do in this situation?' It makes more sense somehow. There doesn't seem much point asking you to fix a situation if that's not what you want to do.

It feels so much better to ask you what you think about a matter and know I'll get an answer straight away.

Does it make you a better person?

Hmmm. I think I'm heading closer to where you want me to be in my life.

But?

I'm still pretty hard to get on with I think. I certainly haven't become 'Mr Popularity'. I am a bit less likely to attack others, but still inclined to say and do things that hurt them.

There's no overnight changing. I think becoming a new person must be a lifelong journey?

It is.

But because I can hear you, then at least I can hear you tell me that, and that makes my stupidity in relationships a little easier to take. But probably not for others. I suspect that even though I listen to you, I'm still a pain for my kids sometimes.

Would you recommend to others that they learn to listen to me?

Only if they are up for a good deal of pain and genuinely prepared to become uncomfortable. If they just want a comfy Christian life they should avoid listening to you like the plague.

How so?

Well, there are no overnight fixes. My Christianity was based on this idea that you came and fixed life's problems. But now that I'm hearing you talk all the time, I'm learning that's not your idea at all. You want to do life with me, not fix life for me. As a result you say a lot of stuff that's very frustrating.

Like what?

Well, you make amazing promises about the key areas of my life that still haven't happened! You promise a great outcome in a particular area and although the evidence that it's happening might be there, it doesn't happen quickly. Some stuff takes years, and still hasn't happened. Some stuff looks like it will never happen.

You're more inclined to say *'It works out fine Mark. You can expect a fantastic outcome. Right now I want you to wait. Be patient. It's worth it.'* **I can't hide my head in the sand about issues anymore. I can't plead 'fix this God' and then just carry on with my life. The more I listen to you the more you gently lead me to working slowly through situations, facing the consequences of my actions. A lot of those consequences aren't pretty.**

So do I talk much about how you've fallen short?

Almost never! I used to think that's all you really thought about when my name got mentioned. How bad I was. But you just don't seem that interested. You've been telling me it's religion and the enemy, 'the accuser of the brethren' that want to focus on my sins. You've told me you don't want me constantly pleading for forgiveness and feeling small.

You make me feel so accepted, and then you want to involve me in fixing what's gone wrong, improving situations etc.

How much of what I say is what you expect, or want me to say?

Not a lot. You often say the opposite of what I want. When I want to do something you say don't. When I don't want to do something you say do.

> *'To what can I compare this generation? They are like children sitting in the marketplaces and calling out to others: "We played the flute for you, and you did not dance; we sang a dirge, and you did not mourn.'*
> MATT 11:16

I'm beginning to realise that verse is about me. I want everything to be tickity boo and sorted. But you don't.

You want to teach me how to be a human by talking me through problems.

You want to *do life with me,* not *fix life for me.* The most painful thing for me about hearing your voice, and it is a pain, is that I'm no longer in control.

> *'The High God rules human kingdoms. He arranges kingdom affairs however he wishes, and makes leaders out of losers.'*
> DANIEL 4:17

I can't get stuck into anything unless you say. And often you say not to get stuck in.

I imagine if a person is not a self-starter you'd be telling them to get stuck in all the time. But me, I want to get stuck in and you say don't.

It makes me feel like I've lost my drive. I'm always having to wait to hear what you've got to say instead of just doing what I want. People who used to like my spontaneous activity, are unsure how to take me anymore. As a matter of fact, even I'm unsure how to take me now that I'm listening to you. Listening to you can be a real pain. But it's also the best thing in the world!

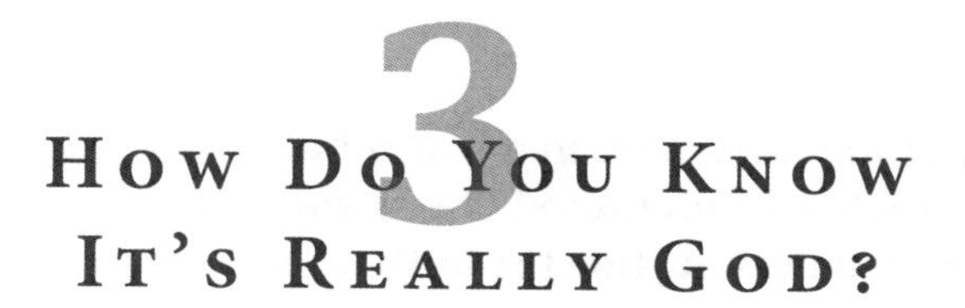

How Do You Know It's Really God?

And why is it a battle to hear him?

So be honest, Mark. What did you think about yesterday's interview with me?

I wondered if I was making it up. I thought 'surely God doesn't just ask questions like a reporter!' And even if you did, how can I possibly hear you that clearly? I had some grave doubts about it.

So what's changed your mind?

A number of people who I respect found it very helpful. They could hear you speaking even if I personally struggled with it.

Is that often the way?

Yes. Often I'm convinced I'm not hearing you. I stop in frustration. Get angry at you. Tell you I'm obviously just making this up. You quietly tell me to continue, but I'm not keen. It often sounds so crazy.

Do you think this is typical?

Yes. Others try this and send me their conversations and it's the same for them. I can see they're hearing God, but they're not sure.

Why do you think that is?

It takes a huge amount of faith to believe you're speaking, straight into our minds just like a man talks to his friend. It's one thing to believe God exists, the Christmas and Easter stories, and then to feel

your presence and direction in a warm but not very specific sort of way. That was what I understood Christianity to be and it takes quite a bit of belief. But nothing like the faith it requires to hear you speak whole sentences, sentence after sentence. That takes huge faith because it seems so crazy. For me it does anyway.

And the enemy is so focused on preventing anyone hearing you clearly.

You wanted to add something else, but you held it in, weren't sure about it. Say it out loud.

Well, my old Christianity, which didn't include a constant back and forward conversation with you, didn't really seem much like faith to me. But I didn't want to say it because that might be knocking others who are content with that.

Why do you think it though?

I lived my old sort of Christianity for 37 years before I started listening to you, and I *know* that listening takes so much faith it hurts, whereas normal Christianity didn't. Not for me anyway.

What do you think the Bible says about a conversation with me?

Paul and David and others said they were always talking to you or hearing from you. Isaiah, Jeremiah, Habakkuk; it was constant back and forward conversation. It's written right there.

But that wasn't my experience. I used to hear from you now and then. Maybe once every year or two. When our little boy had cancer you turned up and talked to us very clearly. Maybe four times in eight months, and that seemed unusually frequent. We acted on what you said and you kept your promise to heal him.

Four times in eight months seemed a huge number of times to hear you speak specifically. Now I hear more than that before I get out of bed in the morning.

You told us to shift from the city to the country to raise our kids. About six years later you told us to shift again. But we heard from you very specifically like that only now and then. The rest was vague impressions.

No one I knew seemed to expect a conversation with you. Occasionally we'd get a strong feeling of direction about our business, or schooling our kids, but not a regular, clearly spoken, conversation.

So aren't you getting a bit big for your boots saying that listening to me all day takes faith, but that Christianity as you knew it didn't?

Well, I don't know. Maybe you can answer? All I know is that the verses in the Bible about faith all centre around listening to you. Not just hearing you when you intervene, but to actively listen to you all the time. That's what the book seems to say that faith is.

> *'So faith comes from HEARING ['akoé: inner hearing, discerning God's voice;] and hearing through the WORD ['rhematos': a spoken word, made by the living voice of Christ].* ROM 10:17
>
> *'It's impossible to please God apart from faith. And why? Because anyone who wants to approach God must believe both that he exists and that he cares enough to respond to those who SEEK [ekzéteó: to seek out, demand, inquire] him.'* HEB 11:6

Strong's Concordance gives a very good interpretation of those verses. I want you to ask me questions and expect an answer. That's what those verses talk about. That you need to believe that I will answer.

Yes and what I always thought Christianity meant doesn't really seem to fit with those verses. Normal Christianity allows your presence to fall, but it doesn't actually 'inquire, or demand' about specifics.

But now I've learned to have a conversation with you, asking you questions and then not 'seeking out' or 'demanding' an answer seems a waste of time. And it doesn't seem to show any faith in you.

Or myself.

Is it easy?

No. It's terrible. You're invisible. Believing you exist is hard enough. Believing you'll answer when I demand an answer is even worse. For me it takes excruciating amounts of faith.

So is that the peak of faith required? To believe that I will respond?

Not for me no.

It gets worse?

I don't know about worse, maybe that's not the best description. But harder. Much harder. For me anyway.

Which bit is harder than believing that I will respond?

That you have responded. Believing that you will respond is a little easier. But to believe that you *have* just about does me in. To believe that I just heard in my mind and wrote down, or spoke out your words, takes a lot of effort for me. I battle constantly with Doubt.

How much? How big an issue is Doubt for you?

Huge. Every single day. All day.

So what do people say about that?

They're sort of incredulous. They ask how can I hear this clearly from God, and then be so filled with doubt?

And?

Well at first, for a couple of years that really phased me because I didn't have an answer. And the doubt Doubt causes is so painful.

So what changed?

You showed me that doubt is absolutely to be expected. Hearing God's voice and Doubt go together. Doubt, the scheming, filthy, slimy, God-mocking, misshapen, disgusting being. The fallen angel.

He always turns up. The moment anyone tries to listen to God he screams orders and he or one of his mini-Doubt slaves are on that person. Immediately.

Why?

Because listening and hearing generates faith as the two verses I quoted earlier say. *'Faith comes by hearing the spoken word of the living Christ'* **That's what the original Greek for that verse means. Faith comes from hearing you speak, and Faith destroys Doubt.**

Anyone who decides to listen to your voice has just declared war on Doubt. And he's serious. War is war. And it's no fun when he attacks.

So what do you when he attacks?

Well, a lot of the time I forget what to do and I get the mental and emotional thrashing of my life. You tell me something really positive, something that gives me huge hope in my situation, but then suddenly I'm racked by doubt. It's like going through a total mental breakdown in a few minutes, or a few hours flat. I imagine it'd be something like mental torture. An inquisition. It makes me want to stop hearing from you. To revert to my old 'not listening to God much' Christianity. Which is obviously his goal. That sort of Christianity is safe for him. When we listen to God, that's not safe for him at all.

So this is a battle?

Absolutely. Listening to you attracts a fight from forces way bigger than me. So then I have to ask you what to do. And you always say to tell him to go.

How does that go for you?

Way better than it did in my old Christianity!!

How come?

Because now, this new Christianity, where I listen to you all the time, he attacks all the time. He's often got me up against the wall, outnumbered and overwhelmed. I can't describe the horror of the torment. I've never experienced anything like it. And of course I don't realize it's him at first. So when I wake up to what's happening it makes me angry. He hits me so hard that I need to fight back just for my sanity. The pain of Doubt's presence gets so agonising that I'll try anything.

His taunts and jabs and mocking are that bad?

I can't describe how bad. The more I listen to you, the more he attacks with clear and vicious lies. And he's horrible to be around. Even before I hear the specific lie, I feel wounded.

So when you tell him to go it works?

Yes. It's not very spiritual. Not many 'in the name of Jesus' sort of proclamations. I'd probably be in trouble with the religious big wigs. But it works.

How do you know?

Because the sudden relief is astounding. I tell him to go, and suddenly it's like you open the window on all that's good.

What about the idea that a conversation with me is deception, so the reason demons disappear when you tell them to go is that you're on the same side?

That's a pretty dumb idea. The Pharisees tried that one on you and you responded with that famous verse.

'And the teachers of the law who came down from Jerusalem said, 'He is possessed by Beelzebul! By the prince of demons he is driving out demons.' So Jesus called them over to him and began to speak to them in parables: 'How can Satan drive out Satan? If a kingdom is divided against itself, that kingdom cannot stand.' MARK 3:22-24

If Doubt is asking me if you have really spoken to me, and I remember to ask you 'is that the filth bugging me?' you say yes. So then I'll say whatever you tell me to say to him. It might be something like *'Stand back!'* **And suddenly it's like a window opens on all that's good in the world and I can see clearly again. Doubt disappears. Gone!**

For good?

No. Sometimes for only five minutes. Sometimes more. Sometimes less. At first I thought maybe I was going properly mad. Doubt one minute, confidence the next. But every time I remember to tell him to go, there is *instant* peace. Whereas madness doesn't have any control over doubt and mental anguish.

But it is a battle. And a battle gets very tiring, and should only be entered into if you're prepared to fight to the death.

OK. That's enough. You need to go to the supermarket with your nephew.

4

What Sort Of Questions Can You Ask Him?

Mark, I want to talk in this interview about the sort of questions you ask me. What sort of questions do you spend most of your day asking me?

Personal ones.

Do you mean private ones?

No. But this is weird. You already know the answer to every question.

Mark, look at the Bible. I ask plenty of questions. I always know the answers in advance, I ask because I want a conversation. Questions start a conversation.

Ok. When I say personal questions, I mean things that aren't big God issues. The conversations I send out to others tend to be you talking to me about some spiritual issue. This interview for instance; the core subject here is 'listening to God'. I'd call that a God issue, as opposed to asking you what I should do today, which is what I'd call a personal issue. Personal is primarily about me, not about you.

Mark, whenever I talk about me it's not really about me at all; it's really about you. It's for your sake.

Well, the answer to your question is that most of the day, the questions I'm asking you are personal ones. Stuff about my life, just my every day life.

And you're obviously relaxed with that? Feel that it's OK by me?

Well, it sure seems to be.

How do you know?

It was the need to ask personal questions that got me listening to you in the first place. I had burning questions about my everyday life. My wife and my kids mostly. I wanted to know what you were saying about our relationships. I'd made so many mistakes, and done so much damage that I realised I couldn't risk doing anything, I couldn't take another step in those relationships without asking you.

Sometimes I still forget to listen to you, and then I almost always mess it up.

I ask questions about my friends, my business, my motorbike, my sore hip, my boat. Just the normal everyday stuff. I ask you about whatever's on my mind.

And instead of ignoring me, you seem eager to answer. You must be because you keep doing it, and instead of feeling all condemned about it, the conversation makes me feel great. You talk about all the stuff that's worrying me. Which, I hope you don't mind, is not a missionary programme or giving to a church, it's how can I be a better man for my family? Or should I be saving more money?

You're also wondering if you should state the second reason. Say it.

Well, the second reason I'm pretty sure you're OK with me asking lots of questions about personal matters, is that verse in the bible.

> *'So here's what I want you to do, God helping you: Take your everyday, ordinary life—your sleeping, eating, going-to-work, and walking-around life—and place it before God as an offering.'*
>
> ROMANS 12:1

That verse says you're interested in my everyday life. And I find that when I ask you questions about my everyday life, you seem more than happy to answer.

Why do you like that?

It destroys that image of you being stuffy and religious and only interested in churchy subjects. It says you're a God who turns up to talk about real stuff. That sort of God appeals a lot more to me than a boring religious sort of God.

No, it's not just you. Everyone hopes there might be a God like that out there somewhere.

That's a relief. I like that you're happy to answer questions about my everyday life because that's what I'm thinking about. It suggests the verse I just quoted means 'live your everyday life asking God what to do in every situation'.

So; most of the time, the questions you ask me, and the things I talk to you about, are personal everyday life things?

Absolutely. I ask you things like what shall I do at work today? Shall I text my daughter and tell her I'm sorry about what I said, or will that make it worse? If you say to text then I'll ask you what to say in the text. And then if that seems to have been the wrong thing, I'll ask you; did I hear that wrong God? And so on.

And I answer that level of detail?

Yes! Sometimes I think I'm making it up. And then I'll tell someone I respect what I think you're saying, even though I'm struggling to believe it myself, and they'll be helped by it and tell me that it was definitely you speaking.

What do you think about suggestions that I'm not interested in such mundane things?

Actually, those suggestions really help me.

How?

Because they're so obviously dumb that they make it much clearer to me that you do want to talk about the little details. Which

supermarket you want me to shop at, whether to get chicken or steak this week. Suggesting that you're not interested in mundane things shows such a lack of knowledge about the Bible. You obviously are.

Why do you say the Bible makes that clear?

Well, it talks about *'if a man is worthy of consideration as an elder, he must be a good husband and father'.* **You're interested in the little details of a person's life.**

Then it talks about a particular wife and goes into detail about how she runs her home, invests in property, works etc. Little details, yet important enough that you want to talk about them.

The Bible even says you count the hairs on my head. And each time a sparrow falls you know. I looked it up. About 13.7 million birds die every day in the US alone. That's a lot of hairs and sparrows! The Bible makes it clear that the little stuff is important to you.

In the Bible you went to all kinds of effort to tell the Israelites about where to put the toilets in the camp. The little stuff interests you.

OK. Last question. How does this relate to your work? Is it actually possible to listen to me about what to do at work?

Yes. You're obviously interested in the little details in every area of my life. Home. Family. Work. If God wants to talk to me about whether to buy Italian Herbs and Spices, or just chilli this week...

You really think I do?

Yes. The same God who talks to me in the supermarket aisle, if I ask his opinion, is the very same God who told me to marry my wife and that he'd save my son and my daughter from death if I got others to pray for them. You're the same God. I can tell. I recognise your voice.

'My sheep listen to my voice.' JOHN 10:27 NIV

Alright, so how does this relate to your work?

I have a conversation like this throughout each day about work. I write down my comments to you and your comments back to me. Just like this. Some of the things you say seem downright stupid, sorry but they do; but they come true. It's incredible.

So what I tell you about work is every day stuff, and short and medium term planning issues like you'd expect to discuss with a partner or a boss?

Yes. Often I feel it's time we got stuck into some project, and you'll say no just wait to see what happens. Or you'll tell me to do a job I think is a waste of time. Or you'll seem to want to focus on my relationship with my staff. You might say I need to inspire them more. Or I'll see something that obviously needs attending to and want to give some orders to that end, but you say just to leave it, because my business partner will tend to it when it's appropriate. And invariably he does. You know what's going on.

If I take the time to ask you, you've got plenty to say about my work.

So that's important; taking the time to ask?

Yes. It seems to be the key. If I don't ask you to talk to me, then you'll only speak when you absolutely have to for my good. You don't push yourself on me. When I badly need direction you'll intervene. For instance when you wanted us to get thousands of people to pray for our son so he didn't die. Or when you wanted us as a family to shift to where we live now. You'll get involved and move things along. But that's not often.

But if I ask your opinion on everything, all day long, then you turn up and talk back. All day long. Just as powerfully as you did when you gave us big direction like shifting homes. You'll actually turn up that powerfully many times a day if I ask. It's unbelievable. And you talk about every little thing. All I have to do is ask, and you speak.

'I sought the lord and he answered me.' PSALM 34:4

'The moment I called out, you stepped in.' PSALM 38:3

Is It Always Clear What God Is Saying?

Mark, listening to a God you can't see is difficult. Is that what you're saying?

Yes. Very. I spend my whole day learning how to do it. All day, every day. Asking you a question, trying to figure out what you're saying. Hearing something in my spirit, then trying to determine whether it was you. All day.

Many people would say that's obsessive, or that God's not that interested.

They do. All sorts of people; from atheists to hi-ranking Christians. They tell me I'm being obsessive and you're just not that interested in talking to us in that much detail. But I suspect that if they found that they could hear the voice of the Creator, they'd get obsessive about it too. And they can. Anyone can. But you already know that.

They say it's not possible to function in life if you're listening to God all day. They say it's too super-spiritual. I thought the same thing at first. But then I decided to experiment. I read a bit of Frank Laubach's book 'Diary of a Modern Mystic' about his tests.

Laubach was a famous missionary to the Philippines. He decided in about 1929 to test whether he could think about God once every minute. He wanted to see what would happen if he did. Would he be better off, or would it stop him functioning effectively in everyday life? He found it made him more effective, more organized, more productive. It amazed him. But it worked.

When I heard that I decided to try something similar. I was already trying to hear your voice all the time because I was in a desperate situation.

But it's not always clear, without any doubt, what I'm saying?

No. Not for me.

So how do you eventually determine what's me and what's not? Can you give examples of how this works, the process you go through to hear me speak?

Yes sure. The most important thing I've learned is that there is a lot of interference. I remember really early on, I was grizzling to you that it didn't seem practical, didn't seem like reality to be listening to you all day. It seemed too spiritual. It seemed impossible.

And what did I tell you?

You explained that I already hear the enemy talking into my mind all day. That he's constantly suggesting negative things, reminding me of hurts, making me feel sad etc. Constant and clear talk from demons. That we really are spiritual beings and we hear spiritually all day long. But we need to choose which spirit we'll listen to.

That made it easier?

Yes because it didn't seem so weird anymore. If I'm already hearing the devil then it makes sense to listen to you instead. If it's just a choice of which spiritual voice I listen to then the choice is obvious. God's voice. And it put me on guard, helped me be more aware of what's going on in the unseen world around me.

OK. So you're saying it's not always clear what I'm saying and that there is plenty of interference from other spiritual voices, demons?

Yes. I never much liked talking about demons. I mean I always knew they existed, but it seemed a bit over the top to talk about them. But yes. They're at us all the time. And when I try to listen to you, they immediately focus on making sure I don't.

Says who?

Says you in the Bible. The very first shot Satan took in this war against us humans was to cast doubt in Eve's mind as to what you'd said. *'Did God really say?'*

But then he made it worse, he started telling her that you were saying and thinking things you weren't. He told Eve that even though you said if she ate from the tree she'd die, that actually you knew that she wouldn't.

Satan wanted Eve to think that you are not altogether truthful.

> *'You will not surely die,' the serpent said to the woman. 'For God knows that when you eat of it your eyes will be opened.'*
>
> GENESIS 3:4-5

He does that to you?

All the time! **He just about drives me mad.**

Is that a good thing though?

Well, in a funny sort of way, yes. It makes me very conscious of how real he is, puts me more on my guard. And it makes me hate him. Trying to hate Satan used to be tough and I guess my belief in him was a bit fuzzy. He's very appealing and seductive.

But now it's easier to hate him, because he's constantly annoying me and frustrating me by trying to make me think you're saying one thing, when actually you're saying the other. The intense frustration of trying to hear you because of his interference makes me genuinely hate him.

There's something else you wanted to say.

Well, listening to you, and hearing you despite all the interference from him, makes me realise how much he hates me. It's as though listening to you has forced him to declare his hand. Forced him to admit that he does exist, really and truly. That there are millions, maybe billions of demons. And that they really do hate you and, consequently, they hate me too.

And that helps?

Yes.

> *'Stay alert! Watch out for your great enemy, the devil. He prowls around like a roaring lion, looking for someone to devour'*
>
> 1 PETER 5:8
>
> *'Now the SERPENT ['nachash': crafty tempter, world power] was more crafty than any of the wild animals the Lord God had made'.*
>
> GENESIS 3:1

Is it OK if I mention a really important point that helps me?

What's that?

I've discovered that your voice will always feel and sound like your voice. *'My sheep hear my voice.'* **But you won't necessarily say things that are what I think you would say. Or even should say.**

You need to explain that.

OK, I'll give a generic example. My kids are too old for this one, but let's say a dad has a problem with one of his kids. They steal something. The dad knows the Bible says to *'spare the rod and spoil the child'.* **He's also read a book by some pastor who says you should whack your kid if they steal. And his own pastor is a stern father and admires other firm dads.**

Now let's say that dad comes to you and asks you, 'what shall I do God?' He's already planning to smack his son, that's not his question, he's asking what else should he do. And let's say that for some reason, in this particular case, you say don't smack him.

That doesn't sound to him like what God should say. It disagrees with his own beliefs, his pastor's beliefs and the books he reads. It does not sound to him like what God should say. But somehow he knows that it's you all the same. Because it sounds and feels like your voice. The words are foreign but the voice is familiar.

So how would that dad know that it was me speaking?

He asks himself does the voice sound and feel like God? *'My sheep know my voice.'*

And how can a person tell that?

It's not always easy. As Eve found out, the enemy is very good at confusion. He tries to make us think his voice is actually you talking. For instance, he loves to pretend that condemnation is actually you.

So give some practical tips on how to determine whether it's me or him?

Well for me, I know that I must always be totally intent on hearing you. Never lazy. Always vigilant. Never just accept the first voice into my mind. Be totally committed to hearing what you say, whether I like what you say or not. Constantly checking if the voice sounds and feels like your voice. It's tough and takes lots of practice.

> *'Be always on the watch, and pray that you may be able to escape all that is about to happen.'* LUKE 21:36

So I might ask you. 'Shall I mention to my daughter the idea of a sailing trip?' And I'll hear 'not right now'. So I might ask 'but you did say to invite her didn't you?' And I might hear 'Yes. You know I did.' All of that might sit fine so I'll go with it. Even though it's frustrating, it sits fine in my heart.

What do you mean 'sits fine'?

Somehow it feels and sounds right. My friend David describes it as a 'satisfaction' that it's God. The voice sounds like your voice and feels like your voice. It sits fine.

OK, but we still haven't talked about interference?

OK, so an example of interference is that I might ask you a question.

Something about a client, something I think I need to advise them. And I'll hear 'yes.'

Now because I know the enemy loves to confuse me when I'm listening to you and because it would be easy to do lasting damage to an important relationship by getting this one wrong, I'll ask a few times, just to be sure. And let's say the answer is clearly yes, you should talk to him.

Well then I'll ask 'should I talk to him about it now?' And often in a situation like that I'll hear 'yes.' But something in my heart might tell me I need to be doubly sure about it, so I ask again, and once again I might hear 'yes', but still feel the need to check is strong. So I'll ask again, and let's say I hear 'no'.

If that happens I get annoyed and a bit confused. I ask which is it? Yes or no?

This sounds incredibly complex, what do you do then?

It is complex! This is a war remember! You said that.

I did.

So I don't give up. I realise that the enemy is involved in either the yes or the no. Which means this issue must be important so I become even more insistent. I ask again; and again if necessary. It's so important to be insistent. If you want to hear God you're going to get resistance, and you have to be prepared to push through it. You have to demand the right answer.

One of the words in the Bible for seek means to demand and to enquire. The issue is how important is it to you to hear God? Not just about that issue, but about any issue? It better be important because if it's not you'll give up before you hear him. In my experience it has to become the thing that drives you above all else. Is that obsessive? Of course! *'Love the lord your God with all your mind!'*

How many times is enough? How many times do you have to ask

before you know you've heard me correctly.

As many as it takes. I have to keep asking until I know in my spirit that I've heard you. One time I sat at the kitchen bench for four hours, alone, shouting at you in frustration. Weeping. Shouting at the enemy. Knowing that I had not heard clearly and peaceably what you'd said. I stuck at it for four hours until I knew absolutely for certain what you'd said.

Why was that particular issue so important?

It probably wasn't any more important than any other issue. What was important was that I knew you had something to say about it because there was so much interference from the enemy. Once he got involved I was then honour bound to keep asking until I heard what you had to say.

> *'ASK ['aiteo': petition, demand] and keep on asking.'* LUKE 11:9
>
> *'the kingdom of heaven has been forcefully advancing, and forceful men LAY HOLD OF IT' ['biazo' laying hold of something with positive aggressiveness]'* MATTHEW 11:12

6 What To Do When You Think God Has Broken A Promise To You

One last interview with Him

A friend of mine, enthused about this idea of listening to God, was sure she heard him say something would happen that week, but then it didn't appear to have happened. She was heartbroken and dismayed. That's part of this experience. We're not used to hearing God, so when we think we hear him and then it appears we haven't after all, our whole world threatens to collapse.

The following is the conversation I had with God on my friend's behalf. I hope it helps you too...

God, I'm wondering what to tell my friend who heard you say that something was going to happen, and then it didn't.

Well. What do you think you should tell them?

God, this is about hearing your voice. It's something that you're teaching me. Isn't it better that I ask you? This is not a subject that anyone seems to know much about and I'm struggling to learn as I go.

I think it would be a good idea if you explain what *you* do when you think I've said something will happen and then it doesn't.

You 'think'? 'Think' doesn't sound very 'God-like', doesn't sound very sure.

'Think' doesn't mean unsure when it's me doing the thinking, Mark. Yes, I think. The Bible makes that very clear. Time and time again. So I 'think' it would be a very good idea if you explain what you do when it looks to you like I've broken my promise.

OK. Well, I panic.

Why?

Because I'm immediately terrified that I don't hear you after all. That these conversations are just make-believe.

Why does that make you panic?

Because my whole life now is based on living for things you've told me to live for. Things I've heard you say direct to my mind. Things that don't seem to have any hope of happening! In pretty much every significant area of my life, I'm only hoping for the outcomes I'm hoping for, because you've told me to do so. The evidence looks to be the opposite of what you've said – so I'm only waiting because you said to wait.

So if it appears that you've misheard me, that either I've broken my promise or you didn't hear me right in a relatively small matter, then you wonder whether I've said any of those other bigger things?

Yes.

So then what do you do?

I demand to know what's happening. I shout at you if I'm somewhere I can. But even if I'm in a crowded room I'm insistent under my breath. I want to know what on earth is going on. I'm desperate. I can feel my world caving in. My world of promises from you, the ones that keep me going, suddenly seems like a house of cards collapsing onto the floor.

How does that make you feel?

Like you've abandoned me.

And yet you demand answers?

That's just human, God! When we feel abandoned by anyone we feel desperate for answers. We feel like we're falling down a hole and we grasp for reality. For answers.

So this must be something that happens regularly? You've got ready answers for it.

Absolutely.

So why on earth would you still try to listen to me if it can often feel like I've broken my promise?

Because so many times I hear you say things that there is no way I could know on my own and yet they come true. So I'm learning. It bends my mind, but I'm learning that us humans really can hear you. If I do, then others can too.

Yes but Mark, you're bitterly disappointed when it seems I've broken my promise. So why persist?

Well I figure, because you're God, that somehow I've misunderstood.

Does that make it any easier?

Not at all. I get angry that you'd let me misunderstand. I feel like maybe you haven't lied exactly, but you've let me down, abandoned me. Left me I guess.

This doesn't sound like a very 'peaceful' relationship with God?

Now you're just winding me up. You know that's what the naysayers tell me. That this can't be you I'm hearing because there's anguish, and anger and I have to keep pressing in to find out what on earth you're saying.

Yes. I want others to know that's what they'll come up against if they persist in trying to hear me. Everyone in the Bible who persisted in trying to hear my voice ended up being out of favour with the very people they thought would be on their side.

OK. Well, the real reason I don't give up when it seems like you've broken your promise, is that I'm desperate. My whole world feels like it's caving in, and I need answers.

You're wondering whether to mention the thing about David in the Bible. Mention it please.

OK, well I remember that David felt like you had broken your promise. Quite often in the Psalms he says things which make me realise he went through this too.

'Will the Lord reject forever? Will he never show his favour again? Has his unfailing love vanished forever? Has his promise failed for all time? Has God forgotten to be merciful?' PSALM 77:7-9

And Jeremiah felt like it too.

'You are right, O GOD, and you set things right. I can't argue with that. But I do have some questions: Why do bad people have it so good? Why do con artists make it big?//Meanwhile, you know me inside and out. You don't let me get by with a thing!'

JEREMIAH 12:1-3

And even you felt like it.

'My God, my God, why have you FORSAKEN me ['egkataleipó': left me behind in dire circumstances]. MATTHEW 27:46

OK. So you feel abandoned, you remember that David, Jeremiah, and even I felt the same, but because you're desperate you persist. You demand to know what's going on. Exactly how do you demand? What's the process? People need to know this, Mark.

It's just something that I've developed out of desperation I guess, but if you think people need to know this; I demand to know what's going on by asking questions.

What questions?

The next obvious question. I ask you something like 'God, did you say that thing I thought you said?' And then I write down, or speak out or even *think* your answer, depending on what's appropriate. It depends on whether I'm on my own or with others etc. And I keep asking that question until I feel that 'satisfaction' that tells me I've heard from you.

How long do you stick with that?

Hours quite often.

Why?

Like I said, if I think you've broken a promise, or I think I've heard you wrong then my world is caving in. So I have to know what's going on.

OK, what's the next obvious question?

If I'm satisfied you said *'yes I did say that'*. **Then the next obvious question is 'well, how come it hasn't happened?' And you might say** *'it has'*. **So I'll ask, what on earth do you mean 'it has'? God, be honest with me 'It hasn't!'**

Explain how you can have such a fluent conversation. This isn't normal for a lot of people. But millions of people want it.

I write down my questions to you, just like I'm doing here, and then write back the answers in faith. It's like prophesying out your answers in writing I guess. Or I speak out, or even think out my questions, and speak back or think back your answers.

And you keep at it until you're 'satisfied' you've heard me. Does that take long?

Yes, when I'm desperate and it seems you've broken your promise,

and I have to find out what's going on, a small conversation can take hours because I'm having to check and recheck your answers until I'm really satisfied that's you talking. You're God. You're invisible. I've had no real training in having a conversation with you, so sometimes it takes excruciating amounts of effort to be sure I've heard you.

And?

And there's opposition. Huge opposition. Satan does not want me fluent in a conversation with you. As I said it's not normal. But you've told me it's meant to be. Which must mean that Satan is viciously opposed.

Some have asked why you think you're so special that God would talk to you like this, or that Satan would pick you out for a beating.

I'm not special. I've messed up so much in my life. Anyone can do this. And if they do you'll answer. And when you do Satan is duty bound to attack. He must, otherwise they'll become dangerous. It spreads, this conversing with you, it spreads like wildfire when the right people hear about it.

So. You stick with asking me the next obvious question, pushing and pushing, not giving up, until you're sure you've got the answers, and it can take hours. How does that make you feel?

The process is exhausting. I'm in tears from the frustration quite often. But the sense of your presence is the most beautiful thing that's ever happened to me. I'm in the middle of a heated discussion, but it's with the lover of my soul, the Creator of the universe, the one who invented me. As Dickens wrote; *'it's the best of times and it's the worst of times.'*

It's like a discussion with the person you love the most. I mean the human person. The person you love the most and you know you can trust. Then suddenly you think they've let you down, broken a promise. Your whole world threatens to collapse momentarily, and yet somehow you know, you hope that they haven't really let you

down. On one hand you're terrified, on the other you're pretty sure you're probably overreacting. But you know you have to ask them for answers, so you do, and you discover that actually you completely misunderstood. They really do love you. They really haven't broken their promise. That's about the best way I can explain it.

Give me some other examples of the next obvious question.

Well, remember I don't give up. I don't accept a vague answer unless you tell me specifically that I have to. So if you say something like *'that thing I promised has happened.'* **I demand the obvious. I say 'what do you mean it's happened?' And I might hear a few words, and I check them. I say 'is that really you'. And on and on it goes. It's like interrogating you.**

Does that worry you? I'm God. People say you can't talk to me like that.

Well, David did, and anyway I'm desperate by that stage. And I'm not prepared to believe in a God who breaks his promises, so it's shoot out time when I think you have. I panic, I go for my guns. I need to know what's going on. And if you're breaking promises then I'll need to change the entire direction of all the significant areas of my life so I have no choice but to do whatever it takes. Either I'm going to get the real answer from you or, abandoned by you, I'm going to have to change direction in every significant area of my life. If that's interrogating God, then too bad.

And you think I'm OK with that?

You seem to be.

I am, Mark. I love it. I designed you for this conversation. Real conversation. Not just the nice stuff. The real stuff too.

I've given you Bible verses that say it's OK. What are they?

'the kingdom of heaven has been subjected to violence, and violent

people have been raiding it.' MATT 11:12

'It is the glory of God to conceal a matter; to search out a matter is the glory of kings.' PROVERBS 25:2

How To Have Your Own Conversation With God

How to deal with doubt

(And answers to all the other FAQs)

How To Have A Back And Forth Conversation With God

THE SIMPLE STEPS THAT NO ONE EVER TOLD US

Try this and you'll soon discover you're talking back and forward with the Creator of the universe. Even people who have been internationally recognised Christian leaders for decades, say that when they try these simple steps, their relationship with God completely changes.

Suddenly they're talking, I mean really talking, with the God they always hoped he was, but were actually a bit afraid to believe was possible.

When they take these steps, they discover they're talking with the Trinity; Father, Son and Spirit; 'those guys'. The crazy thing is that when you talk like this with The Trinity, they'll surprise you. You'll discover they're not the sin-focused, perfectionist God we get taught about.

Instead it turns out that they're the friendly, talkative God who's not religious. They're the Jesus who met the woman at the well, who had lunch at Zachaeus' place, who hung out in Mary and Martha's lounge.

The naysayers, stuck in their religious views, cannot accept the Trinity could be this friendly and accepting. If they accuse you, and say that a conversation with God doesn't line up with scripture, you'll be able to ask God for the exact words to respond, just like Jesus did (ref: John 5:30). It's worth remembering that the Pharisees thought Jesus was promoting ideas that didn't line up with scripture too.

Miriam and I discovered our own separate back and forward

conversations with God at the worst time of our lives, we had just separated after 27 years in our Christian marriage. Suddenly we were face to face with our desperation, it was no longer enough to seek comfort from each other, or our Charismatic, Evangelical religion. Alone, apart, and no longer speaking to each other, we each discovered, in our own miraculous way, that we had no choice but to push through the door and hope against hope that God would speak like a friend. Actually speak in full sentences and paragraphs. We needed more than the nudges and impressions we'd grown used to from the Holy Spirit. We needed human words from God. We needed friendship; no condemnation, no put downs or conditions, just friendship.

It took five long years of learning to hear God more clearly than any other voice, and then, when we least expected it, a conversation with God broke down the walls and showed us the way to start our marriage again.

Until those five dark years, even though we'd been Christians for decades, we didn't know a back and forth conversation with God was even possible. That's what the steps below will make possible for you. A conversation where you can write down, or speak out, sing, dance or even play on an instrument what he says, in full sentences and paragraphs. Modern Christianity doesn't teach this – and yet what on earth is our Christianity if we can't hear God speak even more clearly than the people we live with? God wants someone to teach this, so we're starting the process.

When you've learned it, it's your turn to teach someone else. A conversation with God sets people free, even those of us who thought we were free already. "So if the Son sets you free, you will be free indeed."

HERE'S HOW YOU DO IT: You write your question to God, then write his answer back to you in faith. You don't wait for his answer to come, you just start writing and expect him to give you the words as you write. It sounds crazy we know, but if you try this, pretty soon you'll know you're hearing God. It will overwhelm you that he is prepared to talk this way, so personally and so specifically about your stuff, no matter what your life is like. Which is of course, what he's always been like – prepared to make himself a little lower than the angels that he might talk with us and heal our wounds.

THESE ARE THE SIMPLE STEPS: Write your question to God E.g. "God what are you saying about my job?" Then it seems to help boost your faith when you are first learning this process, to write the beginning of his answer, E.g. "Steve, what I'm saying to you about your job is..."

Then keep writing, expecting God to put the words of his answer into your mind. This is not what the occult call automatic writing, you've still got full control of your pen, just like the writers of the scriptures did when God put his words into their minds.

Writing the start of God's sentence might seem a bit contrived but many find it gets their faith moving and allows God to speak. If you think you're making your answer up, then remember this is a conversation. In a conversation you're allowed to push the other for a clearer answer.

So, if you're not sure if you heard God right, then write that down as your next question to God. E.g. "God, I think I'm making this up."Then write the start of his answer E.g. "Steve, you want to know if you're making this up, what I'm saying about that is..." Then write what comes into your mind – and so on – on and on, back and forth until you're sure you've heard him.

Jesus made it clear that this effort would be required in Luke 11:9. He said we'd need to ask and keep on asking.

How To Deal With Doubt

Doubt's objective is to stop you having your own conversations with God

Doubt called on Eve, and he called on Elijah, Isaiah, Jeremiah, Jesus and Paul. So it makes sense that he's going to call on you too.

WHEN HE ATTACKS, IT WILL BE IMPORTANT TO KNOW A FEW THINGS ABOUT HIM: Knowing these things will help you attack back and win. Doubt is one of the dark one's many names: 'Lucifer', 'Satan', 'Doubt', 'Vindictive', and many other hateful names. He is the inventor of selfishness, and the nature of selfishness is to be consumed with one's self. That's him, consumed with his own putrid nature, consumed with doubt.

He's eternally unsure. He pretends he's sure, but he's not. He makes terrible mistakes, he allowed the crucifixion of Jesus, thinking it was a triumph, only to discover it was his ultimate undoing. He keeps shooting himself in the foot like that, and as a result Doubt doubts himself. And his doubt in himself is increasing. Selfishness is like that, it grows like a cancer.

Doubt is a dark demonic ruler. He is not you, he's a thinking scheming Being. He makes his voice sound like your own thoughts, but those thoughts aren't yours, they're his manipulative lies. When you realise that Doubt's goal is to prevent you having a conversation with God, you're half way there.

He tried to make Eve doubt she could hear God in Genesis 3, by asking her "Did God really say?" He was terrified because he knew when us humans have a back and forward conversation with God we are finally free and immensely powerful. Eve was having conversations with God, and Doubt wanted her stopped before it spread.

Doubt knows that the more we hear God speak, the less we hear Doubt's lies. His lies make us doubt ourselves, whereas faith empowers us. God's voice cancels Doubt's voice and replaces it with faith, Rom 10:17 tells us that "Faith comes by hearing, and hearing by 'the word'". In that verse the Greek for 'the word' is 'rhema' which is best translated 'a spoken word made by the living voice'.

So the second half of the battle is to listen to God's voice, instead of Doubt's, because for many he is too strong to battle head on, at least until they become practised at hearing God's voice. If you try to remove his doubts from your mind, you end up more focused on them. But if you listen to God no matter how loud Doubt shouts, you will begin to hear Doubt less.

Just as when you have a conversation with a friend in a café, the other voices in the café begin to fade. As you become more involved in a conversation with God you'll hear less of Doubt's lies; the lies like, "I can't be hearing this, I'm too sinful." Or "This can't be God, it's just what I want to hear." Or "You're not allowed to hear God direct like this, I must only hear God's voice when I read scripture."

THE WAY TO BEAT DOUBT AT HIS OWN GAME IS: Whenever you find yourself doubting what God has said, doubting that it was actually God, have another conversation with God. Write down something like "Hey God, I'm starting to think you didn't really say that stuff I thought you said this morning. Did I hear you right this morning or not?" And then, don't wait for something to come, start writing and expect him to give you the words as you do.

Scary I know, but it works. Write down what comes in faith. If you're not sure you've heard right, ask again, and then write what comes. And if you're still not sure, ask again, and then write - and again, and again, as long as it takes. Keep at it until you're convinced in your spirit that you've heard God.

WHAT ABOUT LINING UP WHAT YOU HEAR WITH SCRIPTURE?: That's a great idea if you have enough knowledge of scripture (or Google) to know where to look, and understand what you're reading.

But in the same way as you do when you're listening to God direct, you still need to ask and ask to ensure you've heard correctly. That's because hearing God by reading the Bible isn't any more foolproof than listening to him direct. Jesus made it clear that the Pharisees, although expert in the scripture, completely misunderstood it. And Paul scalded the Galatians for relying on scripture, rather than listening direct to the Spirit. That might not fit with popular teaching, but it's right there in the Bible.

There are plenty of examples of this throughout the Bible. In Acts 10:15 God tells Peter to "rise and eat", but Peter knows that what God's telling him to do is not lining up with what scripture teaches in Leviticus 11. So he argues with God, and tells him he's wrong three times. But God says the same thing back, three times. So in the end, after asking and asking for clarification, Peter can feel in his spirit that it is God, he can't quite believe it, but he goes with it. Imagine the strife he must have gotten in with the scripture-mad Jewish Christians when they heard about it. "Doesn't line up with scripture brother, you must be deceived."

Paul got into the same sort of trouble – he heard God say things that didn't line up with scripture too. He heard God tell him it was ok to eat food sacrificed to idols, when scripture forbids it in a number of places, including Numbers 25:2 and Exodus 34:15.

How many times do you need to 'ask and keep asking'? As many times as it takes to know in your spirit that you're pretty darned sure you've heard God. A conversation with God takes practise. Beating Doubt does too. The real question is how badly do you want this?

Does A Conversation With God Have To Be In Writing?

Or can I speak it, think it, sing it, play it, dance it, draw it?

You can do it however you want! But many people find writing the easiest way to start.

A back and forward conversation with God, one like you'd have with a friend, the sort Moses had with God, is different. It isn't normal praying, it's not a one-way monologue most of the time. Normal praying releases power but this is different. A back and forward conversation with God will change everything you know about God. (Rom 12:2) (Job 42:5)

For most of us this is new, even for well known Christian leaders, and many of us find writing our conversations the easiest way to learn. The process is simple – write your question to God and then write back his answer in faith – all it requires is practise. (See 'How to have a back and forth conversation with God').

But there are no rules, we know people who speak their conversation with God out loud. They speak their part and God's part, both out loud. Others do it in their minds, they think their questions to God and think back his answers. They don't wait for them to arrive, but consciously think his answers in faith. Others sing, dance or play their questions to God and his answers back.

There's a reason for communicating God's part of the conversation not just your own. Rather than just hoping God will speak, you grab hold of what he says and articulate it – in writing, speaking, thinking, singing, music, dancing...

God cannot completely reveal himself to us, it would be so overwhelming that we would find ourselves in conversation with him whether or not we wanted. The Bible suggests in Prov

25:2 that he hides what he says but hopes we will uncover it. It's like prophecy, if the person who prophesies decides not to make the effort to speak, then God's words don't come. A conversation with God is like self-prophecy – you interpret the silent words of the invisible God, then write, speak, think, sing, play, dance them to yourself. We found it easiest to start by writing our conversations, many others do too.

What Can I Have A Conversation With God About?

You can ask God about anything you want and expect immediate answers!

We've discovered, that just like a very best friend or that dream granddad, God wants to talk about whatever we want to talk about.

You can have a back and forward conversation with him about your marriage and expect immediate answers; about your job, your business, your finances, your mortgage and your family. Yes, we know Religion has taught us we should be able to use our own minds to figure out most of that, but when you try this for yourself you'll be amazed. You'll discover that God's prepared to answer any question you ask him – he's the one who cares so much about the little things that he counts hairs on people's heads and knows when each sparrow falls.

We have discovered that when we ask him what he wants to talk about, he surprises us with questions of his own – he asks what we want to talk about. This is so far from what we've been taught, that at first we thought we must be deceived, but Christian leaders around the world gave us their stamp of approval.

David talked to God about everything that worried him, Jesus said he did the same in John 5:30 and urged us to come to him to discuss our burdens in Matt 11:28.

You can ask him about your dreams and goals, and your worries, and then write his answer out in faith. He'll put the words into your mind as you write. Ask him about the people you love and the people who trouble you. Ask him which chilli to buy at the supermarket, who to phone today. Take him to work with you and ask his advice all day.

We urge you to try a conversation with God. His responses will amaze you. He doesn't condemn, he's not cross, he's not focused on himself – he's a completely different God than the god of Religion – he's focused on you and whatever you want to talk about.

Why Isn't This Common?

Why isn't a back and forward conversation with God common amongst Christians?

A conversation happens when you speak to another person and expect them to answer you back immediately.

But we Christians don't expect a conversation like that from God. We don't expect it because we haven't been taught to. Our teachers weren't taught either. The Bible is filled with people having a conversation with God, but somewhere in Religion's dark ages, that fact was hidden from us in plain sight.

We've been taught that God won't always respond to a question, and if he does it may take time, and that his response will be in nudges and impressions. Very few of us expect a full conversation with God back and forwards and as easy to understand as talking with friends.

The reason is simple. The Supreme Liar, Satan himself, does not want you to know that you can have a conversation with God. He has used Religion to convince you that you would have to achieve impossible levels of purity and devotion to reach that level of communication with God. He has told you you're not good enough (Rev 12:10) and that only people like Moses are ever going to experience a proper conversation with God. So you settle instead for praying *at* God, and getting impressions and feeling nudges from him, when all the while God wants more than that.

But God will never force himself on us, so if we only expect to hear nudges and impressions, that's all we will hear.

The truth is, that God is speaking to you all the time, in clear sentences and paragraphs "The heavens pour forth speech" (Psalm 19:2). You are already good enough to hear him! You were good enough to die for, "while we were yet sinners Christ died for us" (Rom 5:8) so you're certainly good enough to talk to.

What To Do If God Doesn't Seem To Answer

How to test the spirits (part one)

When you ask God a question and then start writing his answer, expecting it to come, it can feel a bit frightening, like jumping off a cliff and trusting God to catch you.

What if he doesn't answer me? What if I hear him wrong?? Satan will try to frighten you with questions like that, but ignore him and jump into the conversation anyway, God will catch you.

Some people say their mind goes blank and nothing comes, but that's one of Satan's less believable lies. Recognised scientific research has discovered that it is almost impossible for the human mind to stay blank. Google it if you want.

When you ask God a question and start writing his answer in faith, ask him to provide the words as you write, and something will definitely come into your mind. That's an absolute fact. If the thought that comes into your mind is that your mind is blank, then it is obviously a contradiction in terms and is normally your great enemy Doubt.

He asked Eve "Did God really say?", and he loves to taunt you by saying things that sound like your own thoughts. Things like "I knew this wouldn't work", or, "God's not saying anything, my minds gone blank." When he puts those thoughts in your mind, ignore him. Instead, ask God if that thought was from him or the enemy. E.g. "God, the thought that I'm hearing nothing just came into my mind. Did you say that?" And then either just write what comes, or to get yourself started, write something like "Alan, you asked – only write Alan if that's your name – whether the thought that God is saying nothing, was me..." "What I'm saying about that is..." (And then just write what comes in faith). And if you're not sure about the next answer, repeat the process again. Again and again if you need to. 'Ask and keep asking' (Matt 7:7) The Greek suggests 'Demand and keep on demanding'. Your job is to keep asking God until you know you've heard him (1 John 4:1).

What To Do If God's Answer Sounds Too Good?

How to test the spirits (part two)

When we have a conversation with God, it is our job to find out if the answer is really God or not.

"...He lives within you, so you don't need anyone to teach you what is true. For the Spirit teaches you everything you need to know." (1 John 2:27).

It is your job to test the spirits. You do that by asking God again and again until you know that you know you've heard him correctly. If you want a conversation with God, you need to be serious – you need to stick with it long enough to know whether you're hearing him. (Prov 25:2) (Prov 8:17) (Matt 11:12).

Often when you write God's answer, you may find yourself feeling incredulous – can this really be God? The answer you are writing might sound like nonsense or just way too good to be true. Write it down anyway and then immediately challenge God, write your misgivings about the answer as your next question. Eg. "God, I don't think you said that – it sounds like nonsense." Or "God, I think I made that up, it sounds like I'm writing that because that's what I want you to say." Then write down what comes. Do that as often as needed until you are confident you have heard the Spirit establish in your heart what God's actually saying. "Ask and keep on asking." (Matt 7:7).

Yes, sometimes the enemy is able to suggest a thought, and you'll write it down, then feel in your spirit that it wasn't God. When you tell God that in writing, you'll often find that the next answer God will give you is that you're right, that last bit was Satan's interjection.

When that happens, you should feel welcomed to the holy of

holies! Satan was constantly interjecting with Jesus. He even turned up and started talking to the Father when all the angels came to present themselves in the book of Job.

As you can see, a conversation with God is not comfortable Christianity. Are you up for this?

How Often Can I Have A Conversation With God?

Is God really interested in discussing all my boring day to day stuff?

It always surprises us when well-meaning people ask that question.

Yes!! Of course God is interested in your stuff. The Bible says in Rom 12:1 "So here's what I want you to do, God helping you: Take your everyday, ordinary life – your sleeping, eating, going-to-work, and walking-around life – and place it before God." It also tells us in Matt 10:29 "Aren't two sparrows sold for only a penny? But not one of them falls to the ground outside your Father's care. He even counts every hair on your head! So don't be afraid. You are worth more than many sparrows."

God's whole focus is you and your stuff, which is why Satan will try and tell you the opposite all day long – he'll taunt you with stupid thoughts like, "Surely God just wants you to think for yourself? Do you really think God's interested in discussing what sort of Chilli you should buy in the supermarket?" Tell him to bug off. According to the Bible, God is interested in your stuff, and our experience, when we ask him those sorts of questions, is the same.

But don't take our word for it, ask him yourself! Ask him about the little subjects and see what he says, you're going to discover a side of God you didn't know existed. He's interested in everything you are interested in. He's interested in whether your kid's school lunches are what they need to be eating. Do you really think he's too busy to talk to you about your job or your mortgage or your haircut? Of course he's not. But you need to try this for yourself. Ask God direct and then write down his answer (or think or speak it etc.) straight away.

How often can you have a conversation with God? That's a question you should ask God directly. In our experience, whenever we want a conversation with God he is very ready and willing to speak. And the Bible says you cannot wear God out.

Why Is There So Much Doubt And Opposition?

Our advice is don't even start a conversation with God if you don't like the opposition!

If you try a conversation you're going to get opposition, lots of it. This is war. You may already know that as head knowledge, but when you start a conversation with God you will quickly understand the truth of it. Dark unseen forces are viciously opposed to you having a conversation with God. There's nothing closer than conversation, and Satan hates the idea of you being so close to God that you can speak back and forward like friends.

He knows that Religion's methods of praying at God and hoping for nudges and impressions are much safer for him. If you're in actual conversation with God, hearing exactly what he's saying moment by moment, it is much more difficult for the dark forces to herd and direct you. If you attempt a conversation with God, unseen evil will plant constant thoughts of doubt in your mind – "Did God really say that?" "You know you're just making that up." Etc, etc.

Well-meaning people will try to dissuade you too. They'll tell you that the only way to hear God is read scripture, that anything else is dangerous. They've forgotten that Paul warned against that approach many times – google it, but Gal 3:5 is a good place to start. They've forgotten that the Bible teaches we should vigorously demand that God speaks – (Prov 25:2) (Matt 7:7) (Matt 11:12) – and that in John 16 Jesus said he had lots more to say to us but the Holy Spirit would tell us those things when he came.

Others will say it's safer to let God nudge you and give you impressions when he wants, and not to push for more than that. They'll say to 'be at peace and know God's there'. In a human relationship, knowing your friend is there isn't enough, you need conversation. It's the same with God, he wants conversation, and when we speak to him he wants us to expect an answer. (Heb 11:6)

What If I Hear God Wrong?

When you're human, part of listening is getting it wrong

It's no different than when you listen to a friend. Sometimes you misunderstand what they say – even if you write it down.

Part of listening is getting it wrong. If that seems too dangerous, you should take the advice of those religious people who say "Listen to God less and read the Bible more."

The Bible is the written words of God, but putting it above listening to God direct is not what Jesus or Paul taught. They both made it clear they spent more time listening to God than they did reading scripture (John 5:30) (Gal 1:12). Jesus chastised the Pharisees, and Paul the Galatians, for putting the scripture above listening to the Spirit.

So what should you do if you write down something God says to you, then it turns out you heard him wrong? The first step is to ask yourself the following question: Have you ever completely misunderstood what another human said, even when you heard their exact words?? If you can mishear someone you can see, hear and touch, then how much more likely is it you might mishear God who you can't see, hear or touch? And let's say you do misunderstand something another person says – do you stop listening to them? No. Instead you listen even harder when in conversation with them and you ask more questions. It's no different with God. It takes practise to understand what he says, just as it does listening to a friend. You will need to constantly practise listening to God by having back and forth conversations with him. 'Ask and keep on asking'.

For the first 300 years, the early church didn't even have the Bible. All they had were the ancient scriptures. Paul warned that although any scripture inspired by God was good for teaching, if you put them before listening to the Spirit it would bring death

(Gal 3:5) (2Cor 3:6).

The Pharisees knew the scriptures by heart and were convinced that what they read meant Jesus should die! Without a conversation with God you cannot interpret the Bible correctly.

Why Don't I Have To Be A Better Person First?

The two of us have found that whenever we have a conversation with God, we discover again the reality of the Bible's true message – anyone can have a conversation with God no matter what their lives are like. All through the Bible God, and then Jesus, had conversations with people no matter how bad they were, (Cain - *Genesis 4:9*) (Balaam – *Numbers 22:9*), (Rahab - *Joshua 2:8*) (Pharoah – *Genesis 41*) (Nebuchadnezzar – *Daniel 4:31*) (Saul – *Acts 9:5*).

We have discovered that even when we are at our lowest and worst, God seems happy to have a conversation. If we want to ask him questions and then to work out his answer in writing, or any other way that works for us, he'll talk with us.

Why Does God Sound Different Through Each Of Us?

When you try a conversation with God, you'll discover that God sounds a bit like you. And if a friend tries it, then God sounds a bit like them. That's because you're both interpreting the silent voice of the invisible God. If the two of you spoke fluent Mandarin and were interpreting for a Chinese speaker, when you interpreted, the speaker would sound like you and when your friend interpreted, the speaker would sound like your friend. That's because you would both be using your own expressions and turns of phrase to interpret what the Chinese speaker had said.

It's the same when you interpret God's voice, whether you do it in writing, out loud, in your thoughts, in song, play an instrument, dance it, draw it – his voice is being spoken through you, and for that reason will sound or look like you.

Is It Difficult? Will I Need Much Faith To Have A Conversation With God?

Not nearly as much as you'd expect. If you write your question to God and start writing his answer back, expecting him to supply the words, it just seems to come. People who say they thought they had no faith at all, find suddenly they are having a back and forward conversation with God.

It can certainly be frustrating as you go back again and again to God to check what you've heard was really him. If that's faith, then a large part of faith is persistence, but somehow that's an easier concept, a more human concept than the religious ideas that many of us have about faith. And every human is capable of persistence if they want to be. You really do have to keep checking and checking until you're sure in your heart that it's God, but it's so worth it!!

What could be better than hearing God speak direct to you?? One translation puts the faith verse in Hebrews 11:6 beautifully, "Because anyone who wants to approach God must believe both that he exists and that he cares enough to respond to those who seek him." It's not so much super human faith that's required but just believing that God actually cares enough to respond when we seek him.

Important Life Lessons From The Conversations

Hi. These next pages are a few lessons
I have learned in my conversations with God.
I hope they encourage you too

Miriam

Life Is A Smorgasbord

Some things are better left on the table

Smorgasbord is food, heaps of food, you don't need to have all the food, just the bits that you like or are good for you.

I often think that life is a bit like a smorgasbord. All sorts of things are put down before us on life's table – good thoughts and ideas and bad ones too; anger, disappointment, gossipy and unkind thoughts and reactions. We have and we hear conversations with people around us, and of course things happen to and around us. Then we have to decide whether and how we will respond to all that.

I guess the point is that because life's a smorgasbord, we don't have to pick everything up. If someone says something not so nice or you start to react to something in a less than favourable way, make a choice about whether or not you are going to pick that thing up. Sometimes it's better to leave it alone. Much better than picking it up and ranting and raving in its face.

Of course, some things have to be dealt with. Some things, no matter how uncomfortable they make us, really do need to be picked up and sorted out, but I've found it's best to put them back down the moment they're dealt with. It's too easy to keep holding on to them.

Whenever I have a conversation with God about this, he reminds me that the feelings and thoughts and actions we give out are exactly what comes back to us. He'll talk to us whether or not we hold on to things we shouldn't, but the fact remains, it's often better to leave them right there on the table. What we give we are certainly going to receive, so it's good to think about this when we can.

I have found that as I practiced leaving things on the table of life it has become easier to do. The more I do it, the less effort it takes. In fact, to pick up yucky stuff feels really yucky now.

The Better You Choose To Feel The Better You Will Feel

You can have as much control over your feelings as you want to have

Here's something else I've heard God say. He wants us to take charge of the way we feel.

Let's say you wake up in the morning and feel a bit (or very) flat. Before you even have your feet on the floor you feel grumpy, or maybe tired, overwhelmed, anxious, worthless, useless. The truth is, those thoughts don't originate with you. They come from your enemy, who most of all wants to ruin your day. But the good news I hear from God, is that I have control over my feelings and the more I hear this from him, the more I realise that I can deal with this quite simply and successfully.

I have found that first thing in the morning is a time when that old enemy can really get in our ear about all sorts of things and cause a big stir. A lie here, a suggestion there and he gets us all upset. It's not a good way to start any day. He knows that, which is why he does it.

So, just as with the smorgasbord, pick out the bits and thoughts you do like. Pick them up and be thankful for them. Think of the great things about your life – if you are getting kids up for school think about how lucky you are to have kids and a school. Be thankful you can flick a switch and have power for a cuppa and have a hot shower. Be thankful you have a car to take them to school or a bus to put them on, or that they can walk safely there. And so on – work through that day and feel thankful for the good in your life. God keeps telling me the better I choose to feel, the better I will feel. Try it yourself, ask him what he wants to tell you about taking control of your feelings. Write your question to him and write back his answers.

If You Pass Kindness On To Others, They Will Too

You can brighten or darken another's day

This is just a little story that happened to me, one that I've had lots of conversations with God about. It's a simple story but one he's taught me a lot from. It's a story about how our thinking and what we put out there can affect life around us.

I was out driving with a young friend on a lovely country road surrounded by the mountains in Central Otago New Zealand. We were travelling fairly slowly as we had a heavy load on and at the top of a particularly steep hill, my friend pulled over to let a camper van pass that had been following us quite closely. I thought that was very noble of my young friend and felt happy – however my driver then put his window down and out went his fist and fingers and he was not happy.

The van driver looked a bit shocked and carried on up the road. The van then went up the next hill and part way up he slowed to a crawl beside a cyclist and obviously had some harsh things to say to the poor cyclist who in turn shrugged both hands into the air with a 'don't know what that was all about' look on his face. My young driver looked at me and rather sheepishly said "I did that, I did it to the van and then he did it to the cyclist." So it all comes down to the choices we make. If we had chosen to give the van a friendly wave as he passed, he would have then gone on his merry way in a kinder mood.

A Messy Room Is Hardly Life Threatening

God's more interested in a conversation and less interested in what we do wrong

My five kids are all great. I want to talk about one of them here for a minute. This one is good at many things. She works hard at her studies, is great at sport, and is a kind and thoughtful friend. But one thing she wasn't so great at back when this story took place, was keeping her room tidy. Just untidy would have been OK but it was the food and empty glasses and dirty plates.... Anyway, one Saturday morning she came out of her room closing the door quickly behind her and apologising about her room and saying she would give it a good tidy.. sorry sorry sorry...

I told her I was about to walk into town to the supermarket and asked her if she wanted to come... 'yay yes please'. I saw in that little exchange just how God sees us. I love my daughter dearly and what better thing to do than to walk into town with your 18 year old. When you walk you talk. Really her room could wait, I could even help tidy it, it wasn't life threatening. Spending time with her was way more important and fun and lovely.

God sees us the same – yep we're humans – he created us that way so he knows all our downfalls and thoughts and habits - but he's fine with that. He knows stuff will get sorted. What he really wants is to be able to walk and talk with us. The 'messy rooms' will sort themselves out. I didn't want my daughter to keep apologising and talking about how messy she was – I wanted to be able to talk with her about what she wanted to talk about. Our normal human habitual sins are not nearly as big a deal for God as we think they are. Just as we would rather be able to talk to our kids than be always telling them off, God tells me he feels the same about us.

Driving A Kenworth And A Conversation With God

My job on the road teaches me a lot about conversations with God

I was learning a new run from where we live in Tauranga NZ, over the Kaimai range to Te Rapa outside the city of Hamilton. I would be doing this run for two weeks while the usual driver was on leave. I had been assigned a beautiful big cab-over Kenworth truck and trailer tanker unit, and I was really looking forward to driving it. I'd be carting liquid that would be pumped into the five separate compartments in my tankers. The unit was parked on a weigh bridge so we could get the weights right over each axle. I was excited – she was all set up and pumping. We watched the scales above our heads and as they reached a certain weight, we would dash out and open one valve and close another.

We were onto the last compartment when I asked the driver about the site we were unloading at in Te Rapa. I was quite anxious about it as I would only be shown this once and I recalled that there was a bit of a one way system there and I needed to back the trailer into the bay... Suddenly I had lots of questions about all this and was getting myself into quite a stew...

My driver reminded me that actually we were miles from Te Rapa right now and I would be better thinking about what I had to do next. "Shoot – yes – of course, turn off the pump, close the valves, hang up hoses and close lids so I didn't slop product all over the Kaimais.... but Te Rapa??" "Hang on a minute, mate – you've got way more to do before you get there!" "Oh right – pick up paper work otherwise they won't accept my load and send me back for it!" "Yep and then how are you getting out of the Mount? You can't use the toll road or go through Bethlehem so you will have to go past Bay Park, yep and then up the Kaimais and then down the other side. So just think about the 'here and now' so you don't forget anything and everything is done as it should be."

I've thought a lot since that day, well I guess God has told me often since that day that talking with him is a bit the same as getting my big Kenworth and trailer over the hills and across the plains to Te Rapa. He will often give you the big picture – your 'Te Rapa' – but each day we need to ask him what he wants us to do today. We need to expect to hear step by step detail from him. Not just nudges and impressions, that's not good enough when you're moving a big rig hundreds of miles and neither is it good enough when you're negotiating your life through time trying to achieve what God put you here for.

We can only take one step at a time, so ask him what it is for now, for today. One day I was driving that unit down the Kaimais heading to Te Rapa when I got a call from dispatch cancelling Te Rapa and sending me to Reporoa, which is two hours in the opposite direction. Sometimes, once God gets us moving, he will actually give us new directions. So don't worry too much about the big picture and how it will be or how can it possibly be accomplished – just do the next thing and keep the talking going with God – backwards and forwards.

Annette's Story

Don't Give Up

My friend Annette had lots of questions for God. She needed answers. We talked about having a backwards and forwards conversation and she was keen to give it ago.

A couple of weeks later, we talked again about this and she explained, in frustration, that she wasn't getting on very well. She would type out her question then start typing back the answer, but then would feel she was making it up, it was too good to be true, the answer was too simple and so on, so she would hit 'delete' and try again. Frustrated!!

We talked about not hitting the 'delete' button, but to keep writing instead. She did this and although she still had those doubtful thoughts she stuck with it for a bit longer. Then she would walk away from her computer still a bit unsure, and do something else around the house…

Later, Annette would come back to what she had written and was astounded. The words and sentence structure did not actually sound like her after all! She really felt it was God and was very excited.

So don't give up, stick with it. By all means leave it for a time and then come back and read it again. You will be amazed and excited. This is the beauty of writing it down - we can read back over what God has said. And we can question it and discuss it just as we would with a friend over a coffee.

Maggie's Story

The more you practice hearing God's voice, the easier it will get

When I was living in Wanaka, I made four good girl friends – my hairdresser, my neighbour, another heavy machinery operator and then one of those good friends – the mum of my daughter's best friend at school.

Anyway, the daughters introduce us to each other. Her name is Maggie. We exchange phone numbers and day or two later, I receive a phone call "Hi Miri, it's Maggie here. I'm Phily's mum and we met a couple of days ago…" So we chat away and then a few days later, I get another phone call. This time she says "Hi Miri, it's Maggie here..." She doesn't need to tell me who she is because I know who she is. As time goes on and we talk more and more, she no longer even needs to tell me who is calling – because, guess what, I know the sound of her voice! One day I ring her and the phone is answered with "Hi Miri, Maggie here". That didn't sound quite right. The voice was trying to sound like Maggie but something wasn't quite right, and besides, Maggie no longer said that.

So I said to the voice, "Is that you, Phily?" And she came right back with, "Ha you got me – I'll get mum". Sometimes we will hear what sounds right and is almost right, but it's not God. It's the enemy trying to sound like God so that we become accustomed to his voice as well. Once we get used to hearing the enemy's voice and thinking it is God's voice, the enemy can then start telling us the things he wants us to hear from him – his lies, condemnation etc.

So keep practicing at listening and as it gets easier to hear God, you will grow more confident and be more able to push the enemy aside with more assurance.

Ollie's Story

God is talking all the time to us
– we need to learn to listen and talk back

This is a story Mark tells because we were still apart at this stage. Mark was in the process of writing *The Freedom Diaries* and had the manuscript sitting on the kitchen table. Our middle son comes around for a visit with his new girlfriend, Ollie.

Ollie is a beautiful, intelligent, friendly person. She has many beautiful tattoos and a few piercings, lovely long dark hair and bright eyes. She has since become our much loved daughter-in-law and mother of our two grandsons.

Ollie comes into the dining room and sees Mark's manuscript on the table and asks, to our son's absolute horror, "What are you doing here, Mark?" Mark replies "Oh it's nothing" to which Ollie says "It's obviously not nothing! Are you writing a book? Can I have a look? What's it about?" Mark and our son are both a bit panicked – it sounds pretty kooky – a book on conversations with God...

Ollie is insistent and wants to have a read. Mark says she can read the introduction and the first chapter. Ollie takes the manuscript to the outside table, sits down, rolls a smoke and starts reading. And keeps on reading.

Eventually she comes back inside with eyes as big as saucers and makes a profound statement to Mark, one that has taught him so much, "This makes me wonder how many times in my life I have heard God speaking and never knew it was him".

Ollie is a wise young woman and she is so right. God is speaking to us all the time – we just need to become accustomed to listening to him and talking back with him.

PEACEKEEPERS STAY QUIET

AND DON'T ROCK THE BOAT

One morning Mark and I were speaking at a men's breakfast. I was pretty sure I would be the only woman there, and was a bit worried about what I could say that might help all those men.

So I had the following conversation with God in a bit of a panic. The funny thing is that the things he said to me that morning seemed to really help the men at that breakfast, and the thousands of people around the country who I've shared this with since.

"Hi dear God – I'm not sure what you want to say this morning but I have a feeling you have something to say.

Miriam, I want to talk about 'peace keeping'. Peace makers take actions that bring about real peace – but peace keepers stay quiet and don't rock the boat, they don't face issues. It is actually a form of laziness.

You used to keep the peace from the outside – to make things look smoother, you didn't want to upset things – but that was a lie. It stopped you from saying what you thought, stopped you and Mark from communicating and discussing, held you back from learning and growing in your mind and spirit. Keeping the peace is a form of bondage – a way for the enemy to get in and sneakily take control, cause bitterness and discontentment and to take self-esteem from you and cause worthlessness...

So speak up! Speak without bitterness – speak with honesty and genuine love – want the best from and out of each other and for each other – look for good in each other, admire and encourage and build up with words of praise and goodness and kindness. Speak words that encourage the other to listen and to speak also. Ask me for the words to say. Don't be brash and overpowering, be humble and considerate.

Talk, talk and talk. Just as I have told you and Mark to do so, this message is for everyone – not just you two, but it is your message to share with others."

When I married Mark, I had been a nurse, and was now a police constable, so I certainly thought about things a lot and had plenty to say. However, as the children came along, I said less and less and 'kept the peace'. The interesting thing is, that when I read this conversation out in public the first time, Mark told the audience that because I had kept the peace, he had started to think that I didn't love him. He thought I no longer cared enough about him to say what I thought.

Mark and I are still the same two people we have always been – we still have the same personalities, so although coming back together sounds very 'happily ever after', we both need to keep the communication going with each other and with God.

Offence Is More Often Taken

Than it is ever given

Here's a little story about our relationship that seems to really help people. We had been separated for five years, and when this story happened, we'd only been back together about six weeks. I had a job driving a big rig Mack truck and semi, from Mt Maunganui on the beautiful East Coast of New Zealand, six hours up to Portland, just south of Whangarei, and then back again, all in the one shift.

I was on 'day shift' which started at 2.30am. Having just worked six days I was now on my day off. But at 1.30am the alarm went off inside my head and I was wide awake wanting to drive a truck. I got up, folded some washing, answered some emails etc. Eventually I went back to bed in a spare bed so as not to wake Mark, and not wanting him to wake me when he got up.

However, just after 6am, Mark brings me in a cup of tea and thunks it down on the bedside table. Suddenly I was awake again and I thought I'd better get up and look lively. We had breakfast together which was a rather sullen affair. We barely spoke to each other. Mark left for work and asked rather brusquely had I seen the keys to his ute (truck). I told him they were on the table by the front door. I heard him knock them off the table, snatch them up off the ground, and then storm out the door and off down the drive in the ute.

Whew. After he'd gone, I thought to myself that things weren't looking too good – I'd only been back six weeks! Shoot, God, we'll have to do better than this!!! God reminded me that we needed to talk, talk and talk. So I phoned Mark and asked if he'd be home for lunch. He didn't sound very happy but agreed to do so.

When he came in I asked him what was up. He answered,

"Well, you threw the keys at me!" I said I didn't, that he must have knocked them off the table because that's where they were. "Ohhhhh, that's OK then, sorry about that".

Then I remembered I'm not meant to keep the peace, so I asked what the story was with thunking the cup of tea down on the bedside table early that morning. He was sheepish and obviously genuinely concerned and explained that the table in that room was higher than the one beside my bed so in the early morning dark he had fumbled the cup of tea. Well, that was OK then. We had both got the wrong end of the stick.

Two very interesting things came out of that little incident. Firstly, for 27 years, I wouldn't have rung and suggested lunch, nor said anything about what had happened. I would have heard Mark coming up the driveway on the Harley at dinner time, I would have had the house reasonably tidy, kids looking like they were doing their homework, outside chores done etc. Nothing would have been said and we would have just carried on having swept that little altercation under the mat. Not keeping the peace was quite difficult for me to do. And so it would be for many of us 'peace keepers'. There is a time and place to keep the peace, but it shouldn't be kept continually without the peace keeper having a chance to say what they are thinking and how they see things.

The other thing that I learnt was that 'offence is more often taken than it is given'. Neither of us had meant to give offence. The enemy always wants us picking up the wrong end of the stick. He always wants us to take offence. Always. And to look for the wrong in a situation and grab it. That's not how it should be. Talking backwards and forwards with each other – whether it be your partner, child, mechanic, boss, colleague... Don't pick up the wrong end of the stick and take offence. Even when it is given, talking will still help sort out the situation. Talking and listening, talking and listening. Communication is key.

"Let every man be quick to hear (a ready listener), slow to speak, slow to take offence and to get angry" James 1:19

A Few Things We Have Learned About The Conversations

A biblical exegesis to help you in the battle that will come when you have a back and forward conversation with God

A conversation back and forwards with God, is not some add-on to turbo-charge your Christianity. It is the reason that every human was born.

When you try to have a conversation with God you are going to get strong resistance from the enemy and from people, sometimes even people whose opinion you value. That's because, as the Bible points out in Acts 17:28-29, a conversation with God is the reason you were born; "Starting from scratch, he made the entire human race and made the earth hospitable, with plenty of time and space for living so we could seek after God, and not just grope around in the dark but actually find him. He doesn't play hide-and-seek with us. He's not remote; he's near."

The enemy will tell you that you're not good enough and that God's not talking to you. People will tell you that a conversation with God is not scriptural. Which means you're going to have to ask God to reveal to you what he's saying to you direct and to open up the scriptures for you and explain them just like he did to Paul. Paul said we should copy his approach and part of that approach was to listen first to God, second to man. That's how this religious and bloodthirsty murderer became a great man of God – he learned to listen to God direct – "I did not receive it from any man, nor was I taught it; rather, I received it by revelation from Jesus Christ." (Gal 1:12).

A proper back and forward conversation, listening to God speak direct into your mind and heart, is the most powerful experience and able to keep you strong against any kind of attack. When the

Bible says in Hebrews 4:12 that "the Word of God is a two edged sword" the literal translation in the Greek for the term 'Word of God' is a 'divine utterance' or 'Christ expressing the thoughts of the Father through the Spirit'. Because when Paul wrote that, it was still 300 years before the Bible was compiled. All they had was the Jewish Bible and the Septuagint and some of the Apostle's letters and there was a lot of disagreement as to which were authentic and which were not.

The only reliable way for the early Christians to hear God's voice was to listen to him direct; which is why Paul wrote the following in Galatians 3:5 "Does God give you his Spirit and work miracles among you by the works of the law (first five books of scripture), or by your believing what you heard" (the Greek suggests spiritual hearing, discerning God's voice).

For the same reason John wrote in 1:John 2:27; "You do not need that any man should teach you, but the Spirit which you have received teaches you." And John laid the foundations for that earlier in John 16:12 when he wrote, "I still have many things to tell you, but you can't handle them now. But when the Friend comes, the Spirit of the Truth, he will take you by the hand and guide you into all the truth there is."

Clearly, even when reading the scriptures it is important to be sure you are hearing from God, otherwise you can easily think you hear God saying something that he is not. The Pharisees, although expert at scripture, thought God was saying to kill Jesus. The priests in Jeremiah's day thought that God was opposed to Jeremiah's prophecies, and Paul, who was a much more devout Pharisee than most, thought the scriptures required that he kill Christians. So it's no surprise, that once converted, he repeatedly warned Christians that they should not put reading the law before listening to the Spirit.

When it says in Romans 10:17 that "Faith comes by hearing, and hearing by the Word of God", the original Greek says that what is meant by 'Word of God' in that particular verse is 'a thing spoken' or 'the Lord speaking his dynamic, living word in a believer to inbirth faith'. So in short, faith comes as a result of hearing God speak his dynamic, living words direct into us. Which of course, makes a lot of sense. Whenever Jesus spoke direct to someone, their faith grew exponentially.

SO IN SUMMARY: A back and forward conversation with God will change everything you know about God and it will increase your faith more and more rapidly (Rom 12:1-2), how could it not? The Bible heroes and the villains too experienced back and forward conversations with God – it didn't matter to God what their lives were like, he still had a proper human conversation with them (Cain, Balaam, David, Jeremiah, Paul, John, Jesus).

But a back and forward conversation will also attract the ire of the enemy and well-meaning Christians who do not understand it. And a conversation with God takes effort and persistence. Jesus made it clear that we would have to be prepared to "Ask and keep on asking" and to "take the kingdom of heaven by force", and the writer of Proverbs tells us that we are going to have to uncover what God covers up.

Welcome to the conversation, you will never be the same ever again!

What Does The Bible Say About Listening To God?

About hearing him speak into your mind?

About having a conversation where you can understand what he says? About writing down or speaking out his words by faith as he speaks them to you? About this idea that He doesn't find fault but will just talk to you anyway?

The original Greek and Hebrew words shown in the following Bible verses have been sourced from the Lexicon and Strong's Concordance at www.Biblecc.com

> *'Doesn't that privilege of intimate conversation with God make it plain that you are not a slave, but a child?'* GALATIANS 4:7
>
> *'And then he said to me, 'Write this down, for what I tell you is trustworthy and true.'* REVELATIONS 21:5
>
> *'Then the LORD said to me, 'Write my answer in large, clear letters on a tablet, so that a runner can read it and tell everyone else.'* HABAKKUK 2:1-2
>
> *'Now write down this song and teach it to the Israelites and have them sing it'* DEUTERONOMY 31:19
>
> *'The heavens declare the glory of God; the skies proclaim the work of his hands. Day after day they pour forth SPEECH ['Emer': Speech, word. From 'amar; something said]'* PSALM 19:1-2
>
> *'How can a man keep his way pure? By keeping your WORD ['dabar': speech, word]'* PSALM 119:9
>
> *'I have hidden your WORD ['imrah': Command, speech, word] in my HEART [leb: inner man, mind, will,] that I might not sin against you.'* PSALM 119:11
>
> *'For the WORD OF GOD ['logos': speech, divine utterance. Christ*

expressing the thoughts of the Father through the spirit.] is alive and active. Sharper than any double-edged sword, it penetrates even to dividing soul and spirit, joints and marrow; it judges the thoughts and attitudes of the heart.' HEBREWS 4:12

'He sent forth his WORD ['dabar': speech, utterance] and healed them; he rescued them from the grave.' PSALM 107:20

'but whoever LISTENS ['Shama': to hear] to me will live in safety and be at ease, without fear of harm.' PROVERBS 1:33

'I called but you did not answer, I SPOKE ['dabar': to speak] but you did not LISTEN ['shamar': to listen]. You did evil in my sight and chose what displeases me.' ISAIAH 65:12

Gill's commentary says about Isaiah 65:12; 'When Christ called unto them personally, to come and hear him, they turned a deaf ear to this charmer, charming so wisely, and would not attend upon his ministry,'

'So faith comes from HEARING ['akoé: spiritual hearing, discerning God's voice] and hearing through the WORD ['rhematos': a spoken word, made by the living voice]of Christ' ROMANS 10:17

'Everyone should be quick to LISTEN ['akouo': to hear (listen); which comes from 'akauo', properly to hear (figuratively) to hear God's voice which prompts Him to birth faith within], slow to speak and slow to become angry.' JAMES 1:21

'PRAY ['prosuchomai': to pray, exchange wishes; to interact with the Lord by switching human wishes (ideas) for His wishes as He imparts faith ('divine persuasion').] without CEASING ['adialeiptós': incessantly, without any unnecessary interval (time-gap)].' THESSALONIANS 5:17

'So, go now and write all this down. Put it in a book. So that the record will be there.' ISAIAH 30:8

'You keep him in perfect peace whose mind is STAYED [samak: to lean, lay, rest, support] on you, because he trusts in you'

ISAIAH 26:3

'LISTEN ['shama': to hear] to Me, you who know righteousness, A

people in whose heart is my LAW ['Torah': direction, instruction, law];' ISAIAH 51:7

'Do your best to present yourself to God as one approved, a workman who does not need to be ashamed and who correctly handles the WORD ['logos': the thoughts of the Father through the spirit] of truth' 2 TIMOTHY 2:15

The original Hebrew 'Logos' and Strong's Word studies '3056' suggest that 'word' can mean the word spoken by God into our heart, or the words of God spoken to us by others, and probably, although not as obviously, the words of God written down.

'As for you, the ANOINTING ['charisma': anointing, unction, referring to the teaching ministry of the Holy Spirit, guiding the receptive believer into fullness of God's preferred-will] you received from him remains in you, and you do not need anyone to teach you. But as his anointing teaches you about all things and as that anointing is real, not counterfeit—just as it has taught you, remain in him.' 1 JOHN 2:27

'I did not receive it from any man, nor was I taught it; rather, I received it by REVELATION ['apokálypsis': unveiling'] from Jesus Christ.' GALATIANS 1:12

'I am able to do nothing from Myself [independently, of My own accord—but only as I am taught by God and as I get His orders]. Even as I hear, I judge [I decide as I am bidden to decide. As the voice comes to Me, so I give a decision],' JOHN 5:30

Bible Heroes And Villains

And their surprising conversations with God

The model of the Bible is that God will have a conversation with us no matter what we are like. It didn't matter whether the people in the Bible were obeying or disobeying God, he still had a conversation with them.

MOSES

God said to Moses (who had just stumbled on the burning bush and didn't even really know God until this point) "It's time for you to go back; I'm sending you to Pharaoh to bring my people, the People of Israel, out of Egypt."

Moses answered God, "But why me? What makes you think that I could ever go to Pharaoh and lead the children of Israel out of Egypt?"

"I'll be with you," God said. "And this will be the proof that I am the one who sent you: When you have brought my people out of Egypt, you will worship God right here at this very mountain."

Then Moses said to God, "Suppose I go to the People of Israel and I tell them, 'The God of your fathers sent me to you'; and they ask me, 'What is his name?' What do I tell them?"

God said to Moses, "I-AM-WHO-I-AM. Tell the People of Israel, 'I-AM sent me to you.'"

CAIN

God said to Cain (who had just killed his brother), "Where is Abel your brother?"

He said, "How should I know? Am I his babysitter?"

God said, "What have you done! The voice of your brother's blood is calling to me from the ground. From now on you'll get nothing but curses from this ground..."

Cain said to God, "My punishment is too much. I can't take it..."

God told him, "No. Anyone who kills Cain will pay for it seven times over."

JEREMIAH

God said to Jeremiah (when he was still in his teens and hadn't really started being a prophet) "A prophet to the nations – that's what I had in mind for you."

But Jeremiah said, "Hold it, Master God! Look at me. I don't know anything. I'm only a boy!"

God told him, "Don't say, 'I'm only a boy.' I'll tell you where to go and you'll go there.

I'll tell you what to say and you'll say it. Don't be afraid of a soul. I'll be right there, looking after you."

God reached out, touched his mouth, and said, "Look! I've just put my words in your mouth – hand-delivered! See what I've done? I've given you a job to do."

ELIJAH

God said to Elijah (who had just spent days sulking and running away from God) "So Elijah, now tell me, what are you doing here?"

Elijah said it again, "I've been working my heart out for God, the God-of-the-Angel-Armies, because the people of Israel have abandoned your covenant, destroyed your places of worship, and murdered your prophets. I'm the only one left, and now they're trying to kill me."

God said, "Go back the way you came..."

HABUKKUK

Habukkuk complained to God (he was always complaining to God) "What's God going to say to my questions? I'm braced for the worst. I'll climb to the lookout tower and scan the horizon. I'll wait to see what God says, how he'll answer my complaint."

And then God answered: "Write this. Write what you see. Write it out in big block letters so that it can be read on the run."

PETER

(Even when Peter wouldn't accept what God said, God still kept talking to him.)

Then a voice came: "Go to it, Peter, kill and eat."

Peter said, "Oh, no, Lord. I've never so much as tasted food that was not kosher."

The voice came a second time: "If God says it's OK, it's OK."

This happened three times, and then the blanket was pulled back up into the skies.

Then the Spirit whispered to him, "Three men are knocking at the door looking for you. Get down there and go with them. Don't ask any questions. I sent them to get you."

BALAAM SON OF BELEOR

God had a back and forth conversation with Balaam even though he was evil (he was eventually killed by Moses' army for divination in Josh 13:22 and his evil practises were condemned several times in the New Testament – 2 Pet 2:15, Jude 11, and Rev 2:14). Yet God still had a back and forth conversation with him.

Then God came to Balaam. He asked, "So who are these men here with you?"

Balaam answered, "Balak son of Zippor, king of Moab, sent them with a message." (Balaam then explains to God that the men have asked him to curse the armies of Israel).

God said to Balaam, "Don't go with them. And don't curse the others – they are a blessed people."

Other Bible passages about people having a back and forth conversation with God include Jonah when he disobeyed God, Saul on the road to Damascus when he was going to kill Christians, and Job's friends when they counselled him based on their own understanding and not God's.

THE FREEDOM DIARIES:

HOW A LITTLE KIWI BOOK OUT-SOLD ALL THE BIG OVERSEAS TITLES IN THE CHRISTIAN BOOKSTORES

The message about The Freedom Diaries is spreading all over the world! Readers say it changes their lives forever.

The Freedom Diaries is 56 back and forward conversations between Mark Holloway and God.

When Mark's marriage dissolves he screams out to God in terror and to his amazement God speaks back. God has so much to say that Mark has to write it down and he soon realises that either he's going mad or he is actually having a back and forwards conversation with God in writing.

Terrified he is being deceived, he submits his conversations with God to a number of world-recognised Christian leaders who tell him he is indeed hearing from God and encourage him to send his conversations to others.

Soon hundreds are receiving Mark's conversations with God and many urge him to put them in a book. Although reluctant he does so and The Freedom Diaries is born.

The book becomes a best seller and Christians everywhere start exclaiming that their lives have been changed forever by its message.

AND THEN THE BEST PART OF ALL: A conversation with God heals Mark's marriage and family after five years apart. Now Mark and Miriam are teaching the message of the back and forward conversation with God to churches and conferences around New Zealand.

THE FREEDOM ASSIGNMENT

PLEASE TELL SOMEONE!

People everywhere are telling others about The Freedom Diaries. As a result, this message is spreading like wildfire. But we want the whole world to know that anyone can have their own back and forward conversation with God.

That's a big goal we know, but The Freedom Diaries is already a best seller in New Zealand and starting to get read in the UK, Australia and the USA. And it's all because of people like you.

Here are some of the ways you can help spread the message: Tell others about a back and forward conversation with God. Like our Facebook page. Share our Facebook posts. Buy a copy or two of The Freedom Diaries for friends, or buy a set of ten for your church, or a whole box to give away to prisons or drug rehabilitation centres. Helping people discover they can have their own conversation with God changes their lives!

If you would like to buy a box of 40 books to give away email us about volume discounts at: info@thefreedomdiaries.co.nz

If you do those simple things, millions of lives will be changed all over the world.

We plough the biggest part of the profits from the book back into spreading the message but it spreads fastest when you tell your friends and maybe even give away copies of the book.

Mark and Miriam

PS: FREE BONUS! If you'd like to receive special unpublished Freedom Diaries conversations with God, email us at info@thefreedomassignment.com and we'll send them to you free!

MARK AND MIRIAM SPEAKING TO YOUR CHURCH OR GROUP

If you would like us to teach about back and forth conversations with God please email us at info@thefreedomdiaries.co.nz

As more people read The Freedom Diaries and are changed by the message, the demand to have us teach increases. We are always learning more about a back and forth conversation with God – and we love sharing it with people who want to learn more too.

What Church Leaders say about having us teach:

"People came away inspired to spend time with God and confident they could." ***Russell Watts Senior Pastor.***

"People became more hungry to hear from God themselves."

Graham Braddock Elder.

"Only positive feedback from our congregation. Testimony time was amazing, thought it wouldn't stop."

Mark Schonberger Senior Pastor.

Our message includes:

- How a back and forward conversation with God healed our marriage after five years apart.

- How to have your own back and forward conversation with God.

- How to deal with Doubt.

- How to know whether you're hearing God.

- What the Bible says about a back and forward conversation with God, including a look at the Greek and Hebrew texts.

For a FREE INFORMATION PACK please contact:
info@thefreedomdiaries.co.nz